Roths for the Rich

ROTHS FOR THE RICH

HOW TO FUND YOUR ROTH WITH OVER $100,000 EACH YEAR

WILL DUFFY, ChFC

ROTHS FOR THE RICH

How To Fund Your Roth With Over $100,000 Each Year

WillDuffy.com
RothsForTheRich.com

First Edition

Includes bibliographical references.

ISBN 13: 978-1-950486-01-4

I. Business—Investing II. Duffy, Will III. Title

Cover design by Mario Lampic

Interior design & typesetting by Mario Lampic

Disclaimer:

Although the author has made every effort to ensure the information in this book was correct at press time, the author does not assume and hereby disclaims any liability to any party for any loss, damage, or disruption caused by errors or omissions, whether such errors or omissions result from negligence, accident, or any other cause. This book is not intended to provide specific financial or legal advice. The author does not assume and hereby disclaims any liability to any party for any loss, damage, or disruption caused by the information in this book. For advice and guidance specific to your situation, contact Will Duffy or a qualified expert.

Contents

List of Tables

Foreword

Roth IRAs are magical because they help you build tax-free wealth, with minimal government intrusion. Who wouldn't sign up for that? Yet most people are still not taking advantage. I don't get it. Maybe the Roth IRA has just not been explained well enough to make the case. *Now it has!*

In this book you will find the retirement plan you have always been seeking. Financial advisor Will Duffy shows you how to attempt to accumulate the most money possible while paying the least amount possible to Uncle Sam — using the Roth IRA. It's really something everyone should consider taking advantage of. This book seeks to make it easier for you to do that. Will not only makes the case, but he also takes you through possible methods to not only accumulate wealth, but then to potentially hold on to it for life, and even beyond for your heirs.

Follow Will Duffy's simple strategies and you'll be amazed how much you have the potential to sock away tax free by making the tax laws work for you!

You owe it to yourself and your family to attempt to make your savings grow more and last longer. This book shows you how to potentially maximize the benefits of the Roth IRA. You'll want to share this knowledge with everyone you know.

Go ahead now and dig in!

August 3, 2017

Ed Slott, CPA, Retirement Expert
Founder of www.irahelp.com

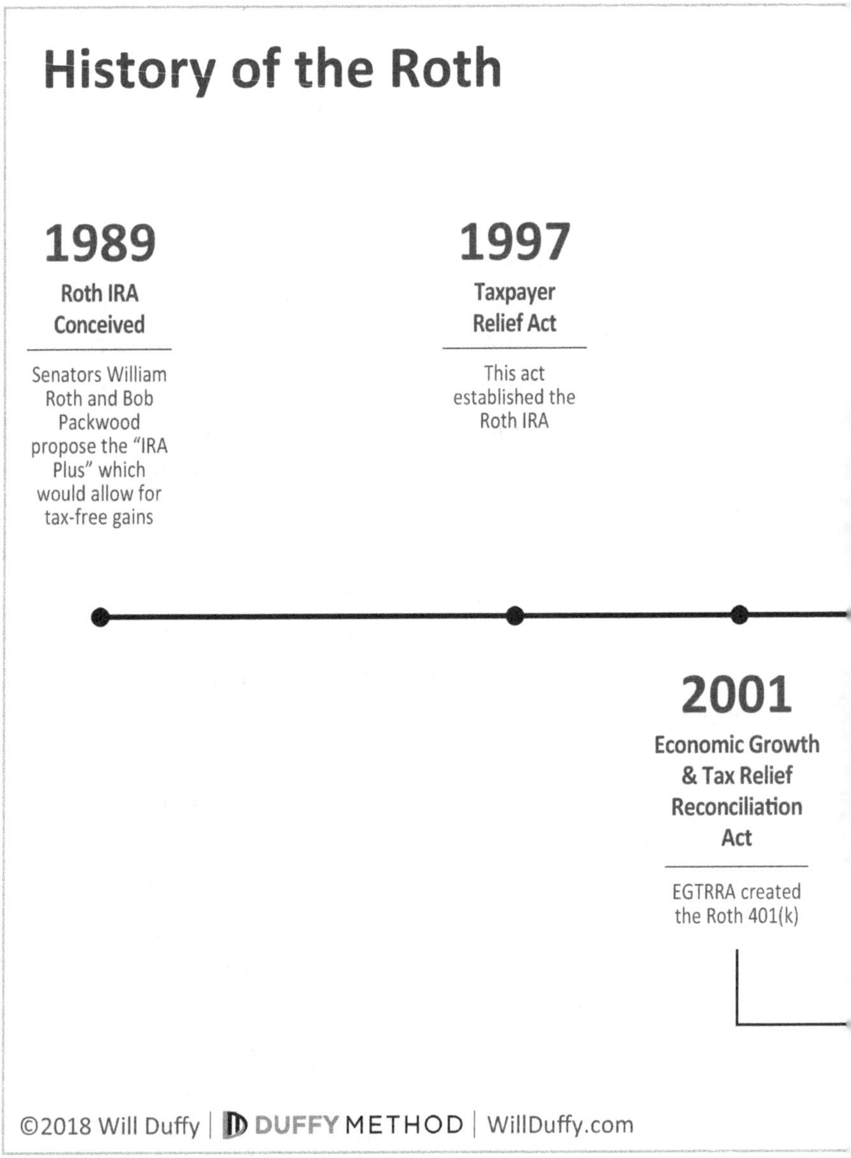
History of the Roth
1989
Roth IRA Conceived
Senators William Roth and Bob Packwood propose the "IRA Plus" which would allow for tax-free gains
1997
Taxpayer Relief Act
This act established the Roth IRA
2001
Economic Growth & Tax Relief Reconciliation Act
EGTRRA created the Roth 401(k)
©2018 Will Duffy | DUFFY METHOD | WillDuffy.com

Figure 1

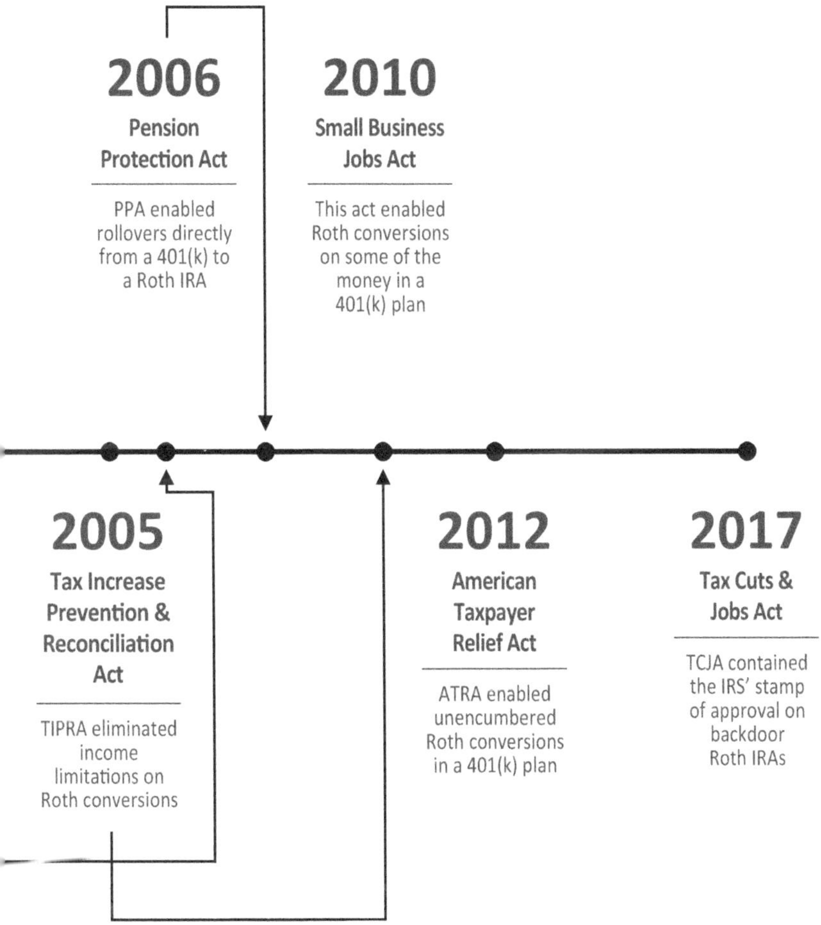

** Arrows indicate when Roth portion of the law went into effect.*

INTRODUCTION

An old gem of folk wisdom expresses my greatest frustration as a financial advisor:

> "It ain't what you *don't know* that gets you in trouble. It's what you *know* that just *ain't so*."
>
> — Mark Twain

My clients are smart, successful, and financially motivated. Even so, they can fall prey to that most universal human snare: the blind spot. Virtually every time I bring up Roth IRAs with affluent investors, they get that look in their eyes. It's a look of dismissal, even derision, as if thinking, *why is he mentioning Roths to me?*

Here's what they *know* that gets them in trouble:

1. I make too much money to contribute to a Roth.
2. Even if I could contribute, the annual allowance is peanuts.

That's where the trouble begins, because what they know "just ain't so." These two points were true of the Roth as it was created 20 years ago. However, six subsequent tax laws have changed everything. (See Figure 1 on page viii.)

In fact, today Roths deliver a giant, golden egg for affluent investors. I assert that Roths offer the second greatest benefit afforded by the U.S. Federal Tax Code.

If you're curious about my choice for the top tax-code benefit, go to RothsForTheRich.com/top5 and download my white paper, The Top 5 Benefits in the U.S. Federal Tax Code.

If you're willing to set aside what you've heard and believed about Roths, I'll show you that it's possible to contribute over $100,000 into Roths every year. And, as amazing as that may seem, it truly represents the tip of the iceberg.

Think of your Roth as one of those colorful, plastic eggs we hide at Easter for children to find. Your investments are what you put into the egg.

What makes this Roth eggshell golden is its seemingly magical power to protect your investment from the devastating effect of taxation. Whatever you can maneuver into that golden shell will not be taxed while your investments grow—regardless of how much they grow—nor even when you decide to take some of your hard-earned treasure out of the golden egg and use it, spend it, or give it away. (We'll get to the rules and details later.)

There's much more to the magical powers of this golden eggshell. Once you are older than 70½, the government won't dictate when and how much you must take out of your golden egg (as they will with most deferred-taxation accounts). Your investments can continue growing, and you can even continue contributing as long as you continue earning!

You may be thinking, *There are still limits with a Roth, right?* Even with the five contribution-maximization strategies I will describe, there are, in fact, limits as to how much you can contribute each year. But what this really means to you is that you will want to diligently take advantage of these extraordinary benefits every single year. Failing to maximize each year's contributions robs you and your estate of extraordinary tax savings and much more.

The potential value added to your nest egg of maximizing your annual Roth contribution is so significant, I will show you ways to do it—even when it seems you lack the cash flow to support it.

If seeing this giant opportunity slip away with each tax year doesn't give you a sense of urgency, perhaps understanding the extraordinary conditions of our present tax environment will make a difference.

The Tax Cuts and Jobs Act of 2017 has created an unprecedented (and undoubtedly temporary) opportunity to capitalize on the power of Roths. This is, I believe, the best overall tax atmosphere we've enjoyed since the creation of the Roth, and I will rigorously argue that it can't last.

Once you understand what I've revealed in this book, you're going to want to give a copy to your CPA, financial planner, and tax advisor. The strategies I describe here are sound, but complex. They are tested, but they can be tricky to navigate. "Don't try this at home!"

If your advisor still thinks Roths are as they were 20 years ago, you need a new advisor. If he or she questions the math, all of the tables are available for download at *RothsForTheRich.com.*

If he or she thinks these strategies are too complicated or not worth the effort, reach out to me. Don't live to regret having missed out on this powerful strategy for potential wealth creation and preservation.

CHAPTER 1

REVISITING SOMETHING OLD, YET NEW

I fault the financial services industry for not educating themselves and their most valuable clients about updated and important developments.

The tax-free Roth IRA and Roth 401(k) may be the most underutilized tax benefits in the tax code. This is mainly due to two widely held misconceptions:

1. If you make a certain amount of money, you can't contribute to a Roth.
2. Even if you could contribute money to a Roth, it's a very small amount.

These were both true when Senator William Roth introduced the Roth IRA, which was signed into law in August of 1997 and became effective in January of 1998. Daryanani Gobind's *Roth IRA Book: An Investor's Guide*, shares his insight:

> I was not happy when we had to phase (Roth contributions) out to incomes of $150,000 for a couple and $95,000 for an individual. But the White House insisted on that. Their argument was that we were helping the rich.

That was then; this is now. Significant law changes since then have unlocked the door to the Roth. These changes allow the rich unfettered access to what I firmly believe is the second-biggest benefit in the tax code, yet few take advantage of it.

To my surprise, two decades later, the great majority of the affluent and rich along with their financial advisors are unaware that the rules of the game have changed dramatically.

Note: Any mention of a Roth in this book refers to both Roth IRAs and Roth 401(k)s. When I specify Roth IRA or Roth 401(k), I am speaking of something that applies only to that one specifically.

How Well Do You Know Roths?

The Roth has now passed the twenty-year mark. Take this quick True/False quiz to see how well you understand Roths.

Do You Know Roths?

True or False

____ The only tax benefit I get with a Roth vs. a traditional IRA/401(k) is that I owe no taxes on the gains in the account.

____ A Roth never has any Required Minimum Distributions (RMDs).

____ The maximum contribution I can put into a Roth (in 2018) is $5,500 ($6,500 if I'm 50 or older).

____ If my income is too high, I cannot make any contributions to a Roth.

____ Since the Roth IRA was created in 1997, there have been no significant changes made to Roths, other than changes to contribution limits and income limitations.

____ I have until 11:59 p.m. on December 31st of each year to make a Roth IRA contribution for that calendar year.

____ Once I reach age 70½, I can no longer contribute to a Roth IRA.

Did you answer true to all these questions? Most of them? Believe it or not, they are *all* false. If you missed any or all of the answers, don't give it a second thought. Very few people (including most financial advisors) truly understand the intricacies—and the extraordinary tax-saving potential—of the Roth.

I fault the financial services industry for not educating themselves and their most valuable clients about updated and important developments. This book solves that problem by clearly explaining the changes in the law that have opened the door for the affluent to take full advantage of the tax-free benefits of Roths.

To keep this book lean and readable, I've taken the step of providing all my supporting documentation online. At *RothsForTheRich.com* you can access tables, calculations, and links to IRS publications and other helpful information.

This book reveals five strategies for contributing large sums of money to a Roth each and every year, no matter how high your income. These methods can enable you to harvest any achieved gains—tax-free! It's highly likely you've never heard about some or most of these strategies.

The Duffy Method also lays out the four most compelling arguments why *everyone* should consider using a Roth over traditional pre-tax tax-deferred accounts. These arguments, largely overlooked in publications on Roths, consist of three facts that can be total game-changers for your retirement and estate planning:

1. Current federal income tax rates are historically low.
2. Roth IRAs don't have Required Minimum Distributions (RMDs) during your life.
3. Roths have higher effective contribution limits than traditional IRAs/401(k)s.

Most of the literature characterizes as controversial the choice to use post-tax Roth vs. pre-tax traditional tax-deferred accounts. With few exceptions, such as donating your IRA to charity, I believe Roths win the debate hands down, especially for the affluent. Under the current tax landscape, there is a clear preference for using Roths.

> **WITH FEW EXCEPTIONS, ROTHS WIN THE DEBATE HANDS DOWN.**

I wrote *Roths for the Rich* specifically for the affluent. The more money you make, the more valuable *tax-free* becomes. Think about it. If someone pays over 50% in federal and state income taxes (such as some who reside in California), to net the same return as in a Roth, they would need to earn double the rate of return in a taxable environment.

I will be discussing large numbers. These numbers represent the upper limits one can strategically get into a Roth annually, and they represent something only the rich can do.

If the numbers seem out of reach, keep one thing in mind: The principles still apply. And the less money one has, the more important it becomes to attempt to preserve it.

One word of warning: *Roths for the Rich* may have a short shelf life. What I'm revealing will likely prompt some in Congress to attempt to change the law and diminish the Roth advantages. In fact, the Obama administration attempted, unsuccessfully, to eliminate two of them. I'll discuss the possible ramifications of revisions to Roths, but don't wait for things to change. A tax-free harvest is still within your reach. Take advantage of what's available today. No one knows what Congress will change tomorrow.

Chapter 2

My Wake-Up Call … to Roth or Not to Roth

Immediately I confronted the two reasons most affluent investors dismiss Roths: income limitations and contribution limits.

When a real estate investment of mine matured a few years ago, I discovered my annualized return was a whopping 30%! My celebration lasted a minute—until I realized the IRS would tax my gains as ordinary income. That would mean I'd pay Uncle Sam almost 45% of my investment gains (the highest federal tax bracket at the time, plus Colorado state income tax). Taxes can be such a killjoy.

I'm not alone. The clients I work with on a daily basis are in a variety of investments. What they experience year in and year out is that a large percentage of their gains would go toward taxes if they didn't have a tax strategy from the get-go. Tax laws are at the mercy of Congress.

> **I HAD TO BECOME MY OWN CLIENT.**

I started researching tax mitigation strategies. When you search for ways to completely eliminate taxes on gains, two options consistently come up: life insurance and Roths.

I love life insurance as a tax-exempt distribution strategy and also for estate planning. But in this case, life insurance wasn't applicable. That left me to explore Roths more closely.

Immediately I confronted the two reasons most affluent investors dismiss Roths: *income limitations* and *contribution limits*. I heard comments like, "I make too much money to have a Roth," or "Even if I could have a Roth, you can't put much more than a few thousand dollars into it."

We are now 20 years into the creation of the Roth IRA. Yet few really understand the dramatic strategies that I will reveal with this book. Signed into law in August of 1997 and available for participation in 1998, it was excluded from anyone who had an income of $95,000 or more ($150,000 married filing jointly) and maxed at a $2,000 annual contribution. That $2,000 limitation became a block for many from using it, including professional advisors. Saving a few hundred dollars in taxes was nominal.

Fast forward to 2018. There have been six tax law changes that have unlocked the ability to use the Roth for individuals earning high incomes. (See Figure 1.) Furthermore, these changes have created the opportunity to invest many times the original $2,000 contribution limit. Yet, the herds that should have driven to do so didn't come.

When I started to make money with my own investments, I had to become my own client.

- How could I strive to protect what I worked so hard for?
- How could I take advantage of tax laws in place and utilize appropriate strategies to my advantage?
- How could my clients maximize something like a basic Roth account into which most believe you can only contribute $5,500 to $6,500 depending upon age[1] — increasing what can be annually contributed by twenty-fold? That increase would definitely get the attention of my clients and their professional advisors.

Was it possible? YES … it was.

---

1 As of 2018 you can contribute up to $5,500 annually into a Roth IRA if you are under 50. Once you reach the age of 50, you are eligible for a catch-up contribution of $1,000, bringing your annual contribution to $6,500. The book will use the following methodology to express the annual limits and ages in a succinct manner: $5,500 ($6,500 > 50).

I've always believed that when the government puts limits on something, it must be good for me and bad for them. If the government doesn't allow the affluent access to something, it likely entails significant tax advantages. That's when, if at all possible, you definitely want to find a way to participate.

WHEN THE GOVERNMENT PUTS LIMITS ON SOMETHING, IT MUST BE GOOD FOR ME AND BAD FOR THEM.

As I continued my search, I kept finding clues that there were indeed ways around most of these restrictions. You've likely heard of some of these tactics, such as *IRA to Roth IRA conversions* and something called a *backdoor Roth.*

As things stand today, here's a quick overview of the basic benefits of Roth IRAs:

- The current cap in 2018 on direct contributions of income to a Roth IRA is $5,500 ($6,500 >50). Contributions may be made retroactively until April 15 of the following year for which they are credited. (You are about to discover how to blast through this $5,500 limitation.)

- Contributions may be made at any age while the owner of the Roth IRA is alive. (Traditional IRAs disallow contributions after age 70½.)
- Contributions, having already been taxed, may be withdrawn at any time without penalty or further taxation. (Contributions to a traditional IRA are, in most cases, assessed a 10% penalty if withdrawn before age 59½.)
- Gains inside a Roth IRA are not taxed while they remain in the Roth and are tax free when they are withdrawn (as long as they are qualified distributions).
- There are no Required Minimum Distributions (RMDs) for a Roth IRA during the life of the owner.
- Under the proper arrangement, a surviving spouse can avoid RMDs on an inherited Roth IRA. (To take advantage of this, it is best to name your spouse as beneficiary on your Roth. This is the cleanest way for your surviving spouse to take the Roth in his/her own name and avoid RMDs for the rest of his/her life.)
- A Roth may be transferred to beneficiaries as an income-tax-free inheritance.

What you've heard about Roths likely doesn't scratch the surface of what my research has uncovered. The *Summa Holdings, Inc. v. Commissioner of Internal Revenue* Court of Appeals case should grab your attention concerning the possibilities of using Roth strategies for tax-free gains. In that case, the defendants turned a $7,000 post-tax contribution into a tax-free gain of over $6,000,000 inside a Roth IRA. The court upheld the use of a Roth in yielding a tax-free return.

My quest for the holy grail of *tax-free* gains has paid off beyond my wildest dreams. I've uncovered methods that have enabled me and my affluent clients to contribute over $100,000 per year to Roths.

I've also discovered the reason the White House in 1997 forced Sen. William Roth to put income limitations on the Roth IRA. When you see the actual numbers and the benefits of the Roth, it will become crystal clear why the government imposed these restrictions. They believed the affluent would discover the massive tax savings—and take full advantage.

While the achievement of tax-free gains has a truly astounding upside, the path to that goal traverses a minefield of sometimes-conflicting tax bills and diverse opinions from respected authorities.

Additionally, an amazing amount of false and misleading information on Roths and related topics gets published—often written by credentialed and respected individuals in the financial services industry. For example, contrary to what author and radio host Dave Ramsey writes in his book *Financial Peace Revisited (pages 154-155)*, you *will* pay taxes on both the contributions and gains when you withdraw from either a traditional IRA or 401(k). He argues that any gains on a tax deferral in a pre-tax vehicle, such as a 401(k), are not ever taxed by the government. This is simply untrue.

Because of the controversies and professional constraints on giving legal and financial advice, this book does not delve into the details of executing any of the strategies I describe. If I got into all of the rules, regulations, and idiosyncrasies of each tactic, it would become thick and tedious and destined for dust and cobwebs.

Instead, I hope to provide an eye-opening tour of the most up-to-date strategies for using Roths to:

- enjoy tax-free treatment of any gains to attempt to build and preserve wealth
- retire free from government-mandated distributions
- invest with the goal of creating a tax-free legacy for your spouse and heirs

I also wish to help you better qualify the advisors who can help you execute these strategies. At a minimum, you will need an excellent CPA *and* an equally competent financial advisor.

Ed Slott, America's IRA expert, has trained hundreds of advisors and is known as the country's best source of IRA advice. You'll find a list of his trained advisors at his website, *IRAhelp.com*. They are members of his Elite IRA Advisor Group. As a member of the group, I can say that I believe the education he provides advisors is second to none.

A Competent Tax Advisor Is Essential

My offices are based in Colorado. One of my affluent clients recently moved to Colorado from California. Their CPA is a well-known, respected accountant located in their former state. As I walked them through one of the Roth strategies available due to a law change implemented more than a decade ago, I was surprised with their initial resistance. You would think this change would have made the rounds by now, since it was passed in 2005.

My clients wanted to verify with their California CPA that what I was telling them was accurate. I couldn't blame them. I'm not a CPA, they had known me for only a few months, and they had a longstanding relationship with their CPA.

We all spoke via a conference call. To my shock, he told them that what I was saying was inaccurate! I quoted the law change from 2005 (which I will detail later in the book)—and he was not familiar with it. Regrettably, he would not acknowledge that he was incorrect in his interpretation. His clients decided he was a wrong fit for their needs and terminated their relationship with him.

Professionals who deal with taxes are working day in and day out with what they are familiar with. The old Roths that were seeded with $2,000 a year weren't viewed as significant. Yet, with the subtle changes in the six tax laws over the past twenty years (See Figure 1 on page viii), the Roth has become a game changer. After all, how would you like to be able to transition from a belief that the most you could invest was only $5,500 as of 2018 to a new understanding that the real amount was actually $55,000 per person every year?

The Duffy Method that I will reveal in later chapters will equip you to create the crucial conversations you need to have with your financial advisors about the impact of taxes on your financial future.

Summing Up

You've worked hard to create your nest egg. You deserve to enjoy the fruit of your labor. A Roth will allow any gains on your investments to grow tax free. The result is that using a Roth in the way I will reveal to you will potentially allow you to invest more toward your retirement.

CHAPTER 3

TAXES: PAY NOW OR LATER?

The #1 thing you should be doing is building your wealth.

Contrary to popular belief, I don't believe that the #1 objective for an individual is to lower his or her tax bill on April 15th. A great deal of that "lowering" has a cost.

The #1 thing you should be doing is building your wealth. Yes, I want you to not pay excessive taxes, but there's more to the wealth-building equation. Do you pay it now or pay it later? In my book *The Other Side of the Coin®: Compound Interest,* I identify the four areas where investors lose:

- Losses in investments
- Investment fees
- Taxes
- Lost opportunity costs when money isn't invested

Meet Jack and Jill

Jack and Jill arrived in my office after an extensive meeting with their accountant. It's year end, and their CPA has advised them to max out their traditional IRAs to reduce their tax bill for the current year. His advice was to add an additional $5,500 in each account for a total reduction to their taxable income of $11,000.

It sounded like good advice, but it's shortsighted. I told them, "You need to look at this financial decision in light of the effect it will have on your entire life ... not just this year." Continuing, I asked, "Do you want an account that becomes worth less, the more successful you become?"

"What do you mean?" Jill asked.

"For example, this IRA might feel like tax savings, but it's not. It is a tax deferral—*deferral* is a fancy word for postpone. You will be postponing the tax to a future unknown rate as well as postponing the tax calculation. By postponing the tax calculation, you will most likely have more money in the account *and* have higher income, so the taxes will be higher."

Jack jumped in. "What else could we do?"

"Don't fund your traditional IRA this year. I suggest you create Roth IRAs instead. You won't reduce your tax bill this year with your contribution. Instead, what you will be doing is reducing your overall tax bill throughout your lifetime. As each Roth account accumulates, any profits acquired from investments will be tax free, and you have the potential for more money that's actually yours to spend.

"I have an idea," I said. "You've told me you have a combined taxable income of $300,000. How would you like to put more than $100,000 in your Roths this year? And if your income continues at this level, how would you like to put in $100,000 plus every single year?"

That got their attention. I went to my white board and revealed the plan.

While today's retirement plan options may seem wrapped in a confusing web of rules, constraints, and competing strategies, one fundamental principle underlies them all: Taxes constitute one of the greatest obstacles to accumulating wealth.

Fortunately, tax-advantaged retirement arrangements can mitigate taxes' devastating effects. These government-sponsored and regulated plans fall into two categories: pre-tax and post-tax[2]. You'll often hear these categories described as *tax-deferred* and *tax-free*, but those terms are misleading and technically inaccurate.

2 There is another term, "after-tax," that is often used when discussing Roth but shouldn't be. "After-tax" refers to dollars contributed to a defined contribution plan that are post-tax and gains are taxed as ordinary income. This will be discussed in more depth later in the book.

> **TAXES CONSTITUTE ONE OF THE GREATEST OBSTACLES TO ACCUMULATING WEALTH.**

Technically speaking, even Roth IRAs and Roth 401(k)s are *tax-deferred* arrangements. Both traditional IRAs and 401(k)s and their Roth counterparts are tax-deferred, which means there are no taxes paid on gains as they occur. Many are confused with this provision. Under current law, the funds in Roth accounts may be withdrawn without tax or penalty when certain conditions are met. But if those conditions are not met, taxes—and sometimes penalties—become due. Since, under certain circumstances, the funds are still subject to taxation, Roths should be categorized as *tax-deferred.*

It's essential for you and your financial advisors to stay current with any tax law changes that impact you and your investments. Today, the current law that permits these funds (including gains) to be withdrawn without owing taxes is subject to change. There's nothing to prevent Congress from imposing additional taxes or changing the rules on these arrangements. If such changes occur, Congress may allow existing Roth accounts to be "grandfathered," or they may determine that all gains after a certain time will be subject to tax.

The debate over pre-tax tax-deferred accounts (such as IRAs and 401(k)s) and their post-tax Roth counterparts isn't about whether we will pay taxes. As Ben Franklin famously wrote, "In this world nothing can be said to be certain, except death and taxes."

We are certainly going to pay taxes. The debate hinges on whether we should fund our retirement accounts with pre-tax dollars or post-tax dollars. One of the themes that I imprint on my clients is:

How to pay tax on the seed only, never the harvest.

It expresses the premise of my argument for funding our accounts with post-tax dollars.

If the money going into an investment vehicle is considered your seed, the money that investment returns becomes your harvest. If you expect your investments to grow, it's far better to pay tax only on the seed and not also on the harvest—especially in today's historically low tax environment.

> IT'S ESSENTIAL FOR YOU AND YOUR FINANCIAL ADVISORS TO STAY CURRENT WITH ANY TAX LAW CHANGES THAT IMPACT YOU AND YOUR INVESTMENTS.

If an investment vehicle can be allowed to grow and compound over time without interruption by taxes, the seeds have the potential to produce a better harvest, even at modest rates of return.

Most advisors and accountants have a built-in aversion to recommending that you pay taxes now, even on the seed of a future tax-free harvest as Jack and Jill's did. It seems more palatable to recommend you take advantage of the immediate tax deductions of traditional pre-tax accounts, rather than pay the tax that would be required to use Roths. They undoubtedly mean well.

They will suggest that by taking the tax savings now, you have more to invest and your nest egg will grow faster. This argument is theoretically correct, but in actual practice it may be a total fallacy, which I will explain in the chapter on Higher Effective Contributions.

Unfortunately, these advisors miss what I call the three "cons" of pre-tax tax-deferment: *contingencies, control*, and *consequences.*

Do you want an account that becomes worth less the more successful you become?

Contingency Planning

The most critical *contingencies* of pre-tax arrangements have to do with future tax rates.

- Will rates go up?
- In retirement, will you remain in the same bracket as in your accumulation years?

Consider the age-old wisdom, *buy low and sell high.* When it comes to tax rates, I advise my clients, "*Pay low and defer high.*" Pay taxes when rates are low and defer when rates are high. In the next chapter, I'll lay out the case for the likelihood of higher tax rates in our future—and the devastating effect they could have on your wealth.

> **A TRADITIONAL IRA OR 401(K) IS ESSENTIALLY A JOINT SAVINGS ACCOUNT FOR YOU AND UNCLE SAM.**

Control Matters

Who *controls* the value of your retirement fund? While you'd like to think you alone make the choices that determine your accounts' future value, I have some bad news. Any money you choose to leave in a pre-tax account, in effect, has a lien on it.

If you choose to keep that money in a tax-deferred account, you have a partner in that arrangement: good ol' Uncle Sam. A traditional IRA or 401(k) is essentially a joint savings account for you and Uncle Sam.

DO YOU REALLY WANT TO GIVE UP CONTROL OVER THE FUTURE VALUE OF YOUR FUNDS?

Now here's the part you really have to think long and hard about: That lien-holding partner gets to unilaterally set the rates (taxes) *and* the terms of that agreement.

Those rates and terms have a direct impact on the value of your accounts. You really have no say in how much of that account belongs to you and how much belongs to Uncle Sam (and his counterparts in your state). *Do you really want to give up control over the future value of your funds?* I would say, "No, you don't."

If you pay taxes today, at least you know the tax you're paying. If you defer paying taxes to the future, you are at the mercy of future lawmakers. To this I cite the old Irish proverb, "Better the devil you know than the devil you don't know."

Consequences Beware!

Finally, there are significant, adverse *consequences* that many advisors overlook when recommending traditional pre-tax strategies. Take the potentially devastating effect of Required Minimum Distributions. In traditional accounts, beginning at the age 70½, the government requires you to withdraw funds *and pay the taxes due*, regardless of whether you need the funds to live on. In a later chapter, I'll reveal the harmful, ripple effect this can have on your wealth.

Any advisor who leaves out such critical information is, like most of the financial services industry, not taking a long view of the situation—and may not be clear about the best interests of their clients.

> IT'S EASY TO GET CAUGHT UP IN THE EXCITEMENT OF TAX-FREE GAINS AND FORGET THAT A ROTH—LIKE ANY VEHICLE—IS USELESS IF THE INVESTMENTS INSIDE IT ARE FAULTY.

A long view necessarily seeks to manage for unknown contingencies, maintains positive control of its assets, and attempts to mitigate potentially negative consequences.

In the spirit of the long view, let me offer a word of caution. It's easy to get caught up in the excitement of tax-free gains and forget that a Roth—like any vehicle—is useless if the investments inside it are faulty.

It's imperative that the underlying investments are not burdened with high fees, as with most mutual funds. Likewise, it's critical to build in down-side protections to avoid losses that take years to recover. Without these safeguards and without a comprehensive approach to long-term growth, tax-free strategies add little value.

Summing Up

Any book on investments, retirement planning, or wealth building that fails to look at the development of these tax-advantaged retirement arrangements *in the context of historical tax rates* would be remiss. When you can visually grasp what has happened in the past, that will enable you to have a much better feel for how the future of retirement strategies may unfold. Throughout *Roths for the Rich*, I will weave those developments and how you may be able to take advantage of them.

CHAPTER 4

HISTORICALLY LOW TAX BRACKETS ARRIVE

Most financial advisors don't want to ask their clients to pay taxes today.

If you are like most Americans, you have grumbled about taxes being too high. Very few, including financial service professionals, truly grasp that we currently have historically low tax brackets. This is a significant reason most fail to take advantage of the tax benefits afforded by a Roth. CPAs love to reduce their clients' annual tax bills, and often this involves deferring some income tax with traditional methods.

> SHORTSIGHTEDNESS IS ESPECIALLY PROBLEMATIC IN THE WORLD OF FINANCIAL PLANNING.

Most financial advisors don't want to ask their clients to pay taxes today, especially their affluent clients in the top tax bracket. Hard-working Americans can't stomach the amount of taxes they are already paying; they are typically looking for any way to reduce the amount they owe. Jack and Jill were no different.

A few years ago, Jack and Jill made a huge mistake. Their financial advisor had suggested an investment to Jack. In turn, he enthusiastically shared with Jill what had been revealed by the financial advisor. As environmentalists, both loved the idea of land conservation. When Jack discovered they could make a combination of an investment that would immediately have an increased value to it, then immediately donate to a vehicle that would generate a substantial increase in overall "paper value" … they would be able to deduct a multiple of what had initially invested. The check was written.

Jack and Jill thought they had found the magic IRS tax-avoidance pill in what was known as a "syndicated conservation easement transaction" that purported to deliver charitable contributions.

They were wrong. It was too aggressive and got the attention of the IRS. Jack and Jill's dubious deduction was disallowed, and they were hit with taxes and penalties. Plus, they lost the original $100,000 they had "invested."

Needless to say, Jack and Jill were unaware of other possibilities. And so was their financial advisor who'd suggested something that was recognized by the IRS as being abused and therefore a listed transaction[3].

YOU SHOULD CONSIDER PAYING TAX TODAY—AND NOT DEFERRING IT.

One of my clients once told me how rare it is to speak with a financial professional who takes a macro-level view—like taking a look at the historical levels of taxation and incorporating them with the client's personal situation. I have to agree with him—this just isn't being addressed widely in my industry. In today's environment, where taxes are at one of the lowest levels in history, it makes dollars and sense to pay taxes now, before they have the opportunity to increase again.

Shortsightedness is especially problematic in the world of financial planning. Throughout *Roths for the Rich* and

3 If you are not familiar with the term *listed transaction*, you probably want to be. The IRS publishes a list of transactions that they have deemed to be similar techniques that they have already determined to be tax avoidance.

the introduction of *The Duffy Method*, I'll recommend you view your finances from a macro level.

I'll also argue that even if you are in the top tax bracket, you should consider paying tax today—and not deferring it. Remember my tax motto: "Pay low and defer high."

> YOU SHOULD *DEFER TAX*
> WHEN TAXES ARE HIGH.

Does this mean that if you're in a high tax bracket, you should defer taxes? No, it doesn't. It actually means you should defer tax when *taxes themselves* are high. As you are about to see, taxes are historically low.

The Creation of Cash or Deferred Arrangements (CODA)

Welcome to Cash or Deferred Arrangements, something that few remember or used. When taxes were high, banks and corporations used a special strategy to reduce taxes. It was a way to pay employees that allowed the employer (the bank or corporation) to take a deduction and at the same time, the recipient (employee) would not have to pay taxes on the payment.

In the 1950s, the top tax bracket was above 90%. That is not a typo. Every year from 1944 to 1963, the top bracket was over 90%. That era of high taxes forced the affluent to strategize how to avoid paying such a high rate. Some people even stopped working! Before Ronald Reagan became the Governor of California and later President of the United States, he was a highly paid actor.

During his presidency, he used to tell members of his White House staff that back in the 1940s, he would loaf around rather than make more than two movies per year, because what good would it do to lose over 90% of it to tax?

Others came up with a way to defer the tax. Banks and large corporations invented something that's now called a CODA, which stands for *cash or deferred arrangement.* These plans killed two birds with one stone. They allowed employers to continue to pay their employees, which meant a deduction at the business level for the corporation. It also allowed the employees to avoid the high tax that would be due via traditional payroll. It was an "everyone wins" environment.

THESE "TAX-DEFERRED" ARRANGEMENTS MADE PERFECT SENSE BECAUSE THEIR TAX BRACKETS WERE SO HIGH.

Here is how it worked: Plans were set up to take part of the income of the employees and pay it into the CODA on their behalf. In other words, it wasn't reflected on their paycheck. And if it doesn't show up on a paycheck, it doesn't get reported on a tax return.

For those who received CODA payments, this was huge. For them, these "tax-deferred" arrangements made perfect sense because their tax brackets were so high. They couldn't really go any higher. So why not defer the tax to the future ... and wait for taxes to come back down at a later date through Congress?

Think about this ... I want to make sure this sinks in. These tax-deferred plans were invented *because* taxes were so high. When taxes are high, it makes sense to defer them. Remember, *pay low* and *defer high*.

The IRS caught on to these schemes (as they always do), and Congress passed new legislation in 1956. They still allowed for CODAs, but under new terms. In 1972, the IRS tried to undo CODAs altogether—apparently it didn't like losing so much tax revenue. But by then, CODAs were very established, having been codified for over 15 years and actively in use. The attempt to undo them failed.

Fast Forward to IRAs and 401(k)s

Along came ERISA—the Employee Retirement Income Security Act that Congress passed in 1974. ERISA grandfathered CODAs until 1977, but more importantly delivered the tax-deferred vehicle known as the IRA.

The IRA made perfect sense in 1974 because taxes were still quite high. From 1965 to 1981, the top tax bracket was 70%! So in 1974, it was a good deal to contribute to an IRA money that would have been taxed at 70% and defer it to the future when taxes would most likely be lower, post retirement.

Imagine for a second that the government had invented the Roth IRA during these high-tax times. No one would have signed up! It made sense to defer the tax for the very reason that taxes were so high.

When 1976 rolled around, Congress passed the Tax Reform Act of 1976, which extended for two years the grandfathering of CODAs. Then Congress passed the Revenue Act of 1978, which created a new section of the tax code. Can you guess which one? That's right, section 401 part (k).

The birth of the 401(k) plan was rooted in the Revenue Act of 1978, which had its roots in CODAs from the 1950s. In 1978, the top tax bracket was still 70%, so it made perfect sense to use a 401(k) plan to defer taxes to the future when the rate would likely be lower.

During these times, no one would have dreamed of a Roth-type vehicle. It wouldn't have made financial sense. Taxes were historically high. So I'll raise the obvious question no one seems to want to ask:

Why are people still deferring their tax when taxes are now historically low?

See *Figure 2* for a snapshot of the history of the top tax brackets.

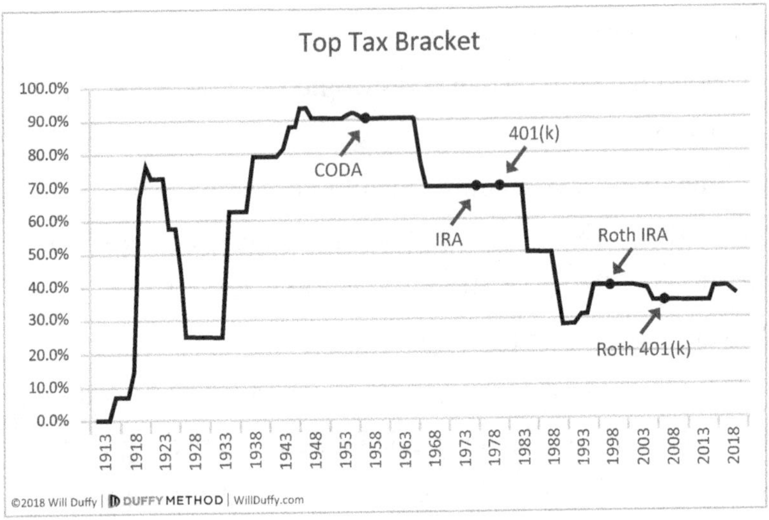

Figure 2

Source: DuffyMethod.com. Ordinary income tax rates peaked in 1944 at 94%. In 1964, they dropped to 77% and in 1965 to 70%. From 1988–1990, they were as low as 28%. With increases and decreases, 2018 brings them in at 37%.

Enter the 1980s. In 1981, Ronald Reagan signed a significant piece of tax legislation called the Economic Recovery Tax Act, also known as ERTA. Starting in 1982, this legislation lowered the top tax bracket from 70% to 50%. This was a hefty drop. In fact, it ended up being too hefty. Tax revenue dropped so much that the government had to figure out ways to increase it. Another law was passed in 1982 to solve the problem. It's common to do an add-on or "clean-up" post a major law. But tax brackets were not increased.

> **REMEMBER, MY ADVICE IS TO *PAY LOW* AND *DEFER HIGH*.**

The next significant change came four years later. Reagan signed the Tax Reform Act of 1986, lowering the top bracket from 50% to 38.5% for 1987. Two years later in 1988, the 38.5% bracket would drop to 28%. These two acts (ERTA of 1981 and TRA of 1986) are commonly known as the Reagan tax cuts.

With the top tax bracket almost at an all-time low (they hadn't been below 50% since 1931), Senators Bob Packwood and William Roth proposed the idea of a post-tax vehicle in 1989. Instead of deferring the tax and getting a tax deduction, a taxpayer would pay the tax at time of contribution, then any gains would be tax free.

This made sense. Taxes were at historic lows. Would they go much lower? They could, but certainly not the massive drop experienced over the previous thirty years. When President George H. W. Bush declared in 1988, "Read my lips: no new taxes," he had to eat his words two years later. Could they increase? Only time will tell.

Remember, my advice is to *pay low* and *defer high*.

The Next Generation: The Roth IRA

Senators Packwood and Roth's idea did not come to fruition until 1997. The Taxpayer Relief Act of 1997 gave us the Roth IRA, and the first contributions could be made starting January 1, 1998. At the time, the top tax bracket was 39.6%—well below the 70% and 90% rates from previous decades.

Historically speaking, traditional IRAs and 401(k)s were created during high tax times. They were right for that time. If taxes are high, it makes sense to avoid paying tax on some of your income and defer it to the future when taxes will likely be lower.

The Roth IRA was conceived when the top tax bracket had dropped to less than one-third of what it was in the 1950s, and less than one-half of what it was in the 1970s. When you look at taxes historically and not just through the lens of today, tax brackets fall into perspective.

Are you ready to learn how Roths can potentially expand your wealth and eliminate that painful bite of tax deferral?

Summing Up

Taxes will always be with us … and you. Many forget just how high taxes were just a few decades ago. It was common for financial advisors to recommend to their clients to defer taxes with the belief that post retirement, a taxpayer would automatically be in a lower tax bracket. Tax law and tax brackets have changed and most likely will continue to change through your life. The traditional "tax deferral" vehicles of yesteryear have become devastating pitfalls.

Chapter 5

Required Minimum Distributions (RMDs)

If you contribute to certain types of accounts like traditional IRAs and 401(k)s, you will be hit with Required Minimum Distributions at age 70½.

In my experience, wealthy clients hate RMDs. It comes as an unwelcome shock when, at age 70½, the IRS requires you to begin withdrawing monies from your traditional IRA or 401(k) plan. Even though you may not need it and would prefer that it continue to grow, the government demands that you withdraw it in amounts they specify and on a schedule they create.

If you fail to comply with these demands, or if the wrong amount is withdrawn, the IRS slaps a 50% penalty in addition to the tax. Ouch.

These withdrawals interrupt your investment gains and the tax reduces your account value. Before these RMDs were withdrawn, your investments had the potential to grow and compound unfettered.

Then the RMD bites a big chunk out of the assets and you can never reattach that missing chunk. Once withdrawn, that chunk no longer grows tax deferred.

If you have a traditional IRA or participated in any 401(k) plan, in order to build a sound financial plan, you must know:

1. The amount you have to withdraw at 70½
2. The tax rate you will pay

Most people have no clue what the amount of their RMD will be or even how to calculate it. And nobody knows what our future tax rates will be.

The Secret Sauce of the Roth IRA

One of the best secrets about Roth IRAs is the *absence* of Required Minimum Distributions (RMDs) while you are living. (RMDs are required on Roth IRAs if a non-spouse inherits them.) This provides your investments with the possibility of growth uninterrupted for the rest of your life.

THE IMPACT OF RMDS CAN BE MORE SIGNIFICANT THAN PEOPLE CAN IMAGINE.

In a traditional IRA or 401(k), the government requires you to distribute your money out of these accounts starting at age 70½. The reason is obvious. They do not want you to defer the tax until you die. Somehow, I believe they think that would be cheating. You can run, but you can't hide.

At 70½, the government essentially forces you to withdraw money from your tax-deferred vehicles so they can get their taxes. What's really scary, they are in full control of the rate at which you must withdraw your funds—*and* the rate at which they will tax you!

Even worse, if you decide not to comply with your RMD, they hit with you a 50% penalty *in addition* to the income tax. And you thought the 10% penalty before 59½ was bad!

The impact of RMDs is more significant than people can imagine. Complex software is needed to calculate its full effect on the long-term growth of your accounts. Fortunately, I have what I believe to be the best financial software in the business, which helped me calculate the numbers used throughout *Roths for the Rich* and with my clients.

> **EVEN IF YOU TAKE THE RMD, PAY THE TAX, AND REINVEST THE REMAINDER, YOU HAVE TWO SERIOUS POSSIBLE PROBLEMS.**

Before we get into the numbers, let's get a big-picture perspective on why RMDs can be so devastating. It's important to understand that the amount increases annually. Each year as you get older, the government requires a higher percentage of the account balance to be distributed.

This distribution hurts the potential for compounding in your investments. This is yet *another* interruption similar to those discussed in my book, *Compound Interest*, the first in *The Other Side of the Coin*® series.

Even if you take the RMD, pay the tax, and reinvest the remainder, you have two serious possible problems.

- First, you have less money available for potential growth because you have had to pay the tax on the RMD. When you pay the tax, your principal is reduced and the result is you have less money than you did before the RMD.
- Second, if you reinvest the money, it cannot go into a tax-deferred vehicle like an IRA or

> Roth. Once it's out, it's out. So you will start paying taxes if the investments grow.

Your tax deferral is gone. Keep reading, and you'll see just how devastating the RMDs have the potential to be. And remember, Roth IRAs do not impose RMDs for you and your spouse while you are living.

There is one more thing worth mentioning even if you feel it doesn't apply to you. These RMDs become part of the formulas for determining the taxation of your Social Security benefit—and the cost of your Medicare premium. In effect, RMDs lower your Social Security benefit (via taxation) and increase your Medicare premium!

Although Jack and Jill are only 40, they need to be aware that RMDs will be in their midst if they participate in a traditional IRA or 401(k) plan.

I asked them, "Do you realize that your actions today can have negative consequences in the middle of your retirement?"

Jill leaned forward. "What do you mean, Will?"

"If you contribute to certain types of accounts like traditional IRAs and 401(k)s, you will be hit with Required Minimum Distributions at age 70½. Few really think about this in their planning years and are surprised to be required to withdraw money at a certain age.

"If you set up a traditional IRA as was suggested by your accountant," I said, "you will have 100% of any withdrawal fully taxable."

Jack shook his head. "That's a surprise neither of us want."

"Here's why you don't want RMDs" I said. "You are required to take money out; the tax rate is set by the government; the amount required to be withdrawn each year increases every year, also set by the government. In other words, you have no say or control."

Jack shook his head. "I don't want that."

"How would you like," I said, "to discover how you can contribute more of your money to Roths than to their traditional counterparts? I will show you how to potentially gain greater control over your financial future with higher effective contributions."

Summing Up

Required Minimum Distributions (RMDs) severely impact your investment decisions. Few really think about RMDs ... 70½ is usually a long way down the road. But when that magic 70½ arrives, your investments can be significantly devastated by mandatory reductions that are out of your control. And those reductions can't be fully reinvested. Few understand what the overall impact of this can have on retirement planning.

Required Minimum Distributions do not help the wealthy. For the Roth IRA owner, not having to withdraw monies means that there can be greater freedom and accumulation. It's a very good thing.

CHAPTER 6

HIGHER EFFECTIVE CONTRIBUTIONS

Those with a traditional IRA have a partner in their account, the IRS ... good ol' Uncle Sam.

One of the biggest reasons to choose a Roth is that you can put more of *your money* into a Roth. This is sometimes referred to as an *effective contribution limit.*

When I asked Jack and Jill if it had ever been explained to them that they could essentially put more money into a Roth IRA over a traditional IRA, they both shook their heads.

"What do you mean?" Jill asked. "Don't they both have the same amounts allowed?"

"No, not really. With a traditional IRA, the government is entitled to a portion of your $5,500, which means you don't have $5,500 of your money working for you. With the Roth IRA, all $5,500 is your money because the government isn't entitled to any of it."

That got their attention.

Moving back to my white board in the office, I began.

"Jack, let's assume that you are Person A. You max out a traditional IRA with $5,500 ($6,500 >50). And let's assume another, Person B, maxes out a Roth IRA, which has the same dollar limit of $5,500 ($6,500 >50).

"Do you as Person A," I asked, "or does Person B have more money in his IRA?"

> **HE WOULD NOT HAVE ANY TAXES DUE, NOR WOULD HE HAVE A PENALTY.**

Jack and Jill exchanged glances. Turning back to me, Jack said, "You know more than we do. Tell us."

"The answer is Person B," I said. "While the dollar amount is the same, Person B is free and clear from taxes on his $5,500. If he chose to walk away from the Roth IRA the next day, he would walk away with $5,500. He would not have any taxes due, nor would he have a penalty because contributions (usually called *basis* in a Roth) are both tax and penalty free—at any time."

> **THE GOVERNMENT NOT ONLY *HOLDS* THE LIEN, BUT ALSO CONTROLS THE *TERMS* OF THE LIEN.**

"Jack, since you are Person A, you have $5,500 in your traditional IRA, but that is pre-tax money. There is essentially a lien on your account—and the government not only holds the lien, but also controls the terms of the lien, which it can unilaterally change at any time! The amount of tax you owe is unknown, as we don't know what the future holds. But the reality remains: You do not have $5,500 of your own money in your traditional IRA, as does Person B in his Roth IRA."

Those with a traditional IRA have a partner in their account, THE IRS. Have you ever noticed that spells THEIRS? Let's assume Person A decides also to walk away from their traditional IRA. What would they get to keep?

> **A TRADITIONAL IRA IS A JOINT SAVINGS ACCOUNT FOR YOU *AND* THE GOVERNMENT.**

Let's assume the year they cashed out of their traditional IRA, their marginal tax bracket was 35%. They would lose $1,925 to ordinary income taxes. That leaves them with $3,575. And if they were under the age of 59½, they would also be hit with a 10% penalty, another $550 hit. That leaves them with $3,025, compared to Person B who has $5,500.

So the effective contribution limit is actually higher with a Roth—because it's 100% *your* money. You can actually put $5,500 of your money into a Roth. With a traditional IRA, the $5,500 represents a combination of your money and the government's. Unfortunately, it's impossible to calculate how much will belong to each. And you have no say or control over what that will be. In essence, a traditional IRA is a joint savings account for you *and* the government.

Some people argue (and rightly so) that if you contribute to a traditional IRA, you will pay less in taxes than if you contribute to a Roth. This is because the traditional IRA contribution is deducted from your income in the year of contribution. While this argument is mathematically accurate, there's a huge flaw in this logic. It's called human nature.

Very few people (if any) actually calculate the tax savings that result from a pre-tax contribution. And almost nobody systematically redirects that savings into investment vehicles. They don't even know where the tax savings are!

I often ask clients, "Where is your tax deduction?" A puzzled look is usually the response.

So I'll ask again. "The tax savings you received from putting some of your income into a 401(k) or traditional IRA, where is it?"

That question always gets a deer-in-the-headlights look. They're speechless.

I tell them it's nowhere to be found. It doesn't exist anymore. Is it in their 401(k) or traditional IRA? Nope. Let me explain.

When someone deposits income into a pre-tax vehicle, like a 401(k) or traditional IRA, that money is deducted from their income when they do their taxes the following year. If someone wanted to calculate the exact tax savings they received, they would need to wait until the next calendar year and have their CPA or tax preparer run two tax returns: one with the income deduction and one without.

> THE EFFECTIVE CONTRIBUTION LIMIT IS ACTUALLY HIGHER WITH A ROTH—BECAUSE IT'S 100% YOUR MONEY.

Comparing the tax paid on the two returns would tell you exactly what their tax savings were. At that point, one would have to transfer that tax savings out of their bank account (assuming it's not already spent) and into an investment. How many times do you think people do this? In my years of investment guidance for the wealthy, I've never heard of anyone doing this. Not one. People max out their plans and hope for growth. It's a "set it and forget it" mentality.

The mathematical examples in *Roths for the Rich* assume that traditional and Roth accounts are maxed out and that no other money is saved and invested from the tax savings on the traditional side. Out of curiosity, I did run numbers assuming the savings are invested—and the Roth *still* wins. All my spreadsheets are available for download at my website, *RothsForTheRich.com.*

There are two reasons the Roth still wins.

- First, we are in historically low tax brackets.
- Second, Roth IRAs, unlike traditional IRAs, do not have RMDs.

The facts make a solid argument for considering using Roths today, no matter your income.

- You can put more of your own money (effective contribution) into a Roth IRA or Roth 401(k).

- Tax brackets are historically low.
- Roth IRAs do not have RMDs.

Summing Up

Once you understand the 'dollars and sense' of the differences with a Traditional IRA and a Roth IRA and then incorporate it with your present and projected incomes, you will grasp why contributing 100% of your money initially may yield more money for retirement years.

The reality is, you can't put $5,500 ($6,500 >50) of your own money into a traditional IRA and think it's all yours; the government is always included because of the deferred tax issue. With a Roth IRA, what you put in is what you take out, plus or minus gains/losses. Of course, in either case, if you withdraw monies before 59½, there are penalties on the gains. However, with the traditional IRA, penalties for early withdrawal apply also to contributions.

The next section will look at the bottom line: the numbers. You will see how powerful this vehicle can be from an actual money standpoint. And the final section will explain how you, an affluent person, can take advantage and use Roths—despite the hurdles you may believe will prevent you from doing so.

CHAPTER 7

THE NUMBERS

You have to crunch the numbers and have someone reliable, knowledgeable, and up-to-date on tax laws.

Jack and Jill are now asking questions that relate directly to them. They are young—both 40. He earns $300,000 a year. They want to reduce their current tax obligation yet are deeply interested in increasing their assets and what they will have when they eventually retire.

"You said that we could put more money in than the standard $5,500," Jack said. "Can we talk about that? In our case, what would those numbers look like?"

"Yes ... how does ten times that amount sound: $55,000 per year that you could put away, Jack? For example, let's assume you put $55,000 each year in a Roth beginning now at age 40, and you do so every year until you retire at 65. Let's also say you live until age 90. The result is that you could potentially have almost $9 million more than if you had put $55,000 annually into a SEP-IRA."

"Tell me more ..."

All my spreadsheets documenting the assumptions I used in these calculations are available for download at *RothsForTheRich.com.* But first, an important disclaimer: The hypothetical scenarios below are for illustrative purposes only. There can be no guarantee that any investment strategy will achieve its goals and all investing involves risk. Every hypothetical financial scenario on the planet has problems. That's because there are too many variables, and with time, these variables will undoubtedly change.

Also, everyone's situation is unique. This means you need to take any hypothetical financial scenario as just that: hypothetical.

Roth vs. Traditional

This first example will underscore the fact that RMDs can be devastating for non-Roth accounts. We will look at a contribution of $55,000 a year into both a traditional account and a Roth account. This $55,000 number, known as the *415 limit*, will probably increase in the future. But for 2018, $55,000 represents the limit for any defined-contribution plans. I'll show you later how to reach this limit each year with a Roth.

If a 40-year-old started contributing $55,000 a year into these accounts and did so for 25 years and retired at 65, then lived to age 90, the following results would happen with an 8% investment return. (The percentage return of 8% is purely arbitrary and really irrelevant, because it's the same for both the traditional and the Roth examples.)

At age 90, the Roth account would have a balance of $29.7 million.[4] The other two accounts would have a combined balance of just $21.1 million[5] as seen in *Figure 3*. This is almost a $9 million difference! I hope I have your attention now.

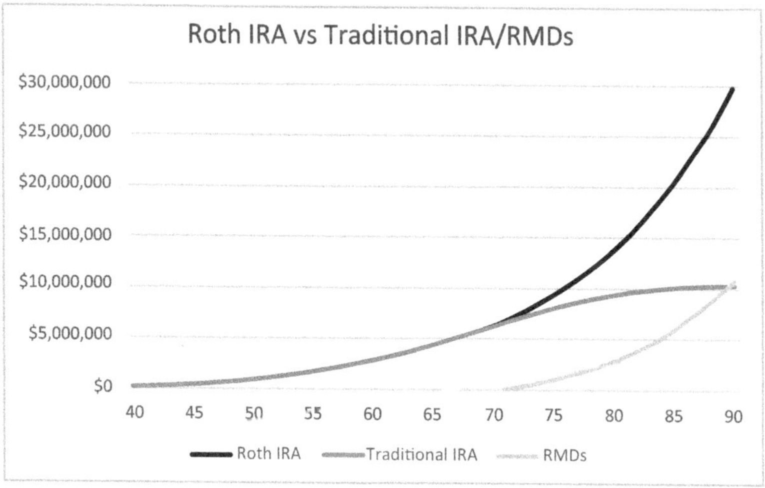

Figure 3

4 $29,739,454

5 $9,544,659 + $11,581,343 = $21,126,002

Let me explain what's going on. The biggest factor is RMDs. On the traditional side, RMDs are taken out at age 70½, the tax is paid (37%), and the remainder is reinvested in a taxable account, which also grows at 8%. The combination of the taxes paid, and the hit taken in the taxable account each year is brutal.

So there are now two accounts on the traditional side. One is an IRA, and the other is a taxable account. The traditional IRA is worth $9.5 million,[6] and the taxable account is worth $11.6 million.[7] The reason for the two accounts is that the RMD *must* be taken out of the IRA each year—and in this example the net amount after taxes is reinvested.

But the combined $21.1 million in the two accounts still has more taxes due! The $9.5 million in the traditional IRA will be taxed as ordinary income when it is inherited by the next generation. And the $11.6 million in the taxable account is still subject to both ordinary income and capital gains taxes.

With all the variables, calculating the remaining tax is not easy. But to give you an estimate, if the IRA were taxed at 37% (today's top bracket, which is historically low) and just the stocks in the taxable account were taxed at 20%

6 $9,544,659

7 $11,581,343

(today's top long-term capital gains tax bracket), the net amount would be just $16.8 million.[8] After taxes in this example, that represents almost a $13 million difference between the traditional accounts and the Roth.

A $13 Million Difference

This is an apples-to-apples comparison. The same amount is invested to both the traditional IRA and the Roth IRA. Each account grows at the same rate. And you end up with a difference of almost $13 million.

The reason can be summed up in one word: *taxes*. Now you know beyond a shadow of a doubt why the government has a vested interest in preventing the rich from taking full advantage of the tax benefits of a Roth. The tax benefits can be significant!

Withdrawing Income

Let's now consider the effect of withdrawing income. Instead of the money just accumulating in these accounts, at age 65 I will begin withdrawing income from them. This comparison will match the gross income on the two sides. If we withdraw $100,000 from the traditional IRA, we will also withdraw $100,000 from the Roth. The same gross distributions will take place on each side.

---

8 $10,822,867 + $6,013,135 = $16,836,002

Safe Withdrawal Rates

If the same $55,000 is invested each year from age 40 to 64, the balance in both the Roth and the traditional IRA is $4.3 million.[9] This amount will be the same because the contribution limit is the same for both traditional and Roth accounts, and both sides are being maxed out equally. But you are making higher effective contributions to a Roth, because all of it is your money. In this example, the difference is not seen on the *accumulation* side, but on the *distribution* side.

A 3% distribution rate at age 65 calculates to $130,000.[10] This means that the first year I will withdraw $130,000 from each account (traditional and Roth) and increase that withdrawal each year by 3%. (It's important to note that at age 65, I lowered the investment return from 8% to 5%. People who want income from these accounts to last the rest of their life typically put a portion into fixed-income investments, which theoretically lowers the overall return. Again, I have done this on both sides, giving us a fair comparison.)

9 $4,342,493

10 $130,275

> What I have included here is beyond the scope of this book. My intention is to write an entire book on the topic one day, but I will use a 3% distribution rate at age 65 with an annual 3% Cost of Living Adjustment (COLA). Safe withdrawal rates and distribution rates are something almost no one has been taught, and this can be devastating for those who hope to one day retire.
>
> Calculating 3% at age 65 and increasing that dollar amount by 3% per year is a commonly accepted safe withdrawal rate for stock market-based investments. It's called safe because the chances of running out of money before death are very slim, regardless of the sequence of returns the market provides after retirement. However, as with all investing, there are still risks, and no investment strategy is guaranteed to be "safe" or meet its objectives.

Spendable Income

The first significant item to note is that the Roth side provides much higher *spendable* income. Because no taxes are due, all $130,000 can be spent and enjoyed. The traditional side has income taxes (both federal and state, though the calculations in this book consider only federal.) Those federal taxes, if paid at today's top bracket of 37%, result in an annual spendable income of only $82,000.[11] Compared to $130,000, that $82,000 represents almost a 40% decrease in income to spend and enjoy.

If we look forward all the way to age 90, the Roth account provides $4.7 million[12] of spendable income, compared to just $3 million[13] of spendable income from the traditional IRA. That's over $1.7 million dollars more income to spend and enjoy in retirement as seen in *Figure 4.*

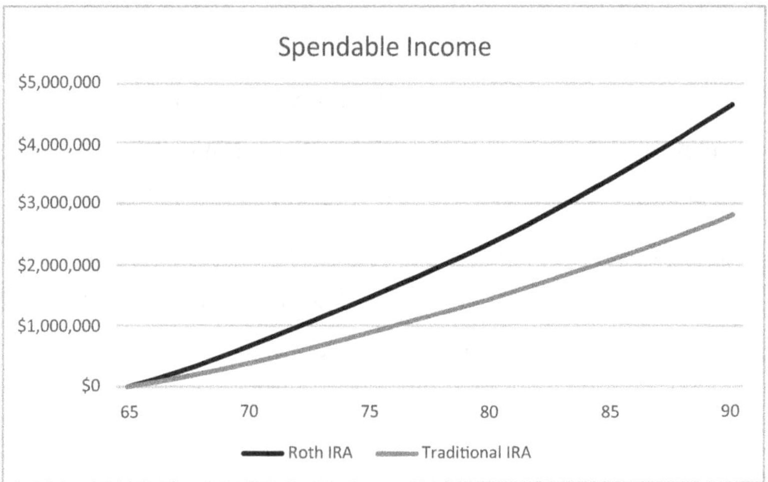

Figure 4

11 $82,073

12 $4,749,723

13 $2,992,325

And the balance that remains in the Roth account at age 90 is $5.9 million.[14] But the traditional accounts (IRA and taxable account for RMD reinvestment) total just $5.1 million[15] as seen in *Figure 5*. And remember, taxes will still be due on that $5.1 million! After taxes are paid on the traditional side, that represents another potential $1.5 million difference.

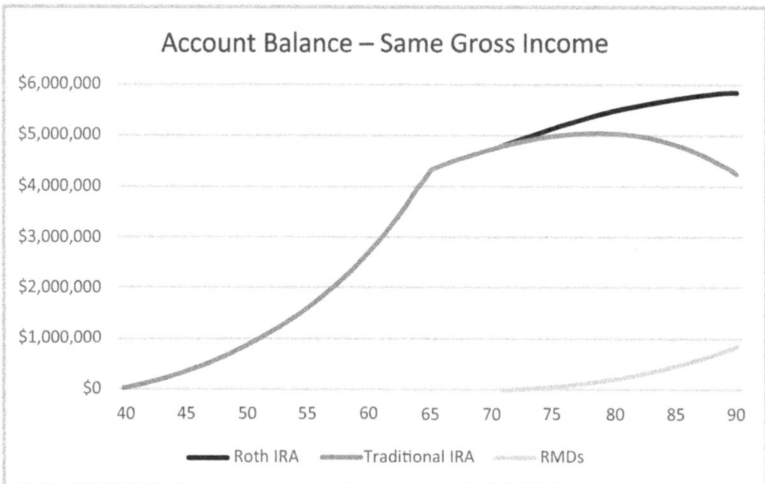

Figure 5

14 $5,864,737

15 $4,270,356 + $842,896 = $5,113,252

Required Minimum Distributions

I'd like to point out that in this example, the income (3% at 65; increased by 3% each year) does not fully satisfy the RMDs in the later years. That is how big RMDs can grow. They can exceed the rate of safe withdrawal. Unfortunately, this fact has not been accounted for in models of safe-withdrawal rates. Later in life, this can lead to serious problems for people who plan to follow widely accepted rates for safe withdrawal. They may very well run out of money.

Equalizing Spendable Income

Let's look at another example. This time, we'll make the *spendable* income equal on both sides. If we have $130,000 to spend on the Roth side, we will withdraw enough on the traditional side to net $130,000 to spend after taxes. This will blow you away!

The cumulative *spendable* income on both sides will be the same: $4.7 million. From a lifestyle standpoint, the results are identical. So where is the main difference in this scenario between pre-tax and post-tax? It comes in the account balance at death. (In this example, I'll assume death happens at age 90.) To cover the taxes on the traditional side, more money was withdrawn to net the same spendable income as on the Roth side. So this account will clearly have less money. How much less? You'll be *shocked*.

The Roth, as we showed above, has $5.9 million at age 90. But all that remains in the traditional account is $673,000[16] as seen in *Figure 6*. That's not a typo. Not even $1 million. And that remaining amount has yet to be taxed!

This represents a difference of almost $5 million. And I'd like to point out that in this calculation, no RMDs were required. That is because the withdrawals each year were higher than the minimum currently required by the government. So the RMD was satisfied each year by the gross withdrawal from the account.

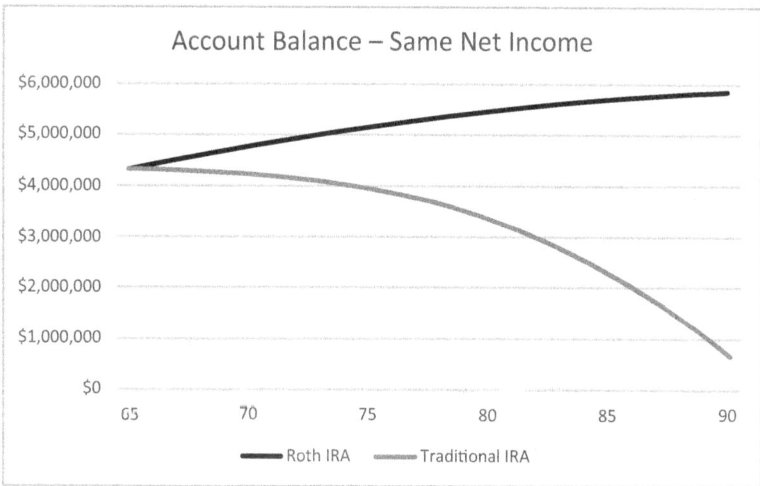

Figure 6

16 $672,706

A Roth at Retirement

I hope you've seen enough evidence to convince you of the potential power of the Roth. It's compelling. But I want to give one more example to show you that converting to a Roth—even right before retirement—may be worth considering. A lot of people think if they've reached retirement and never included a Roth in their financial plan, it's too late. I disagree.

We will compare a traditional IRA worth $2 million at age 65 with someone who took their $2 million IRA at 65 and converted it to a Roth in one lump sum. This means they have only $1.3 million[17] in their Roth, because on the conversion they paid over $700,000 in income taxes. Roth conversions generally make more sense when spread out over multiple years. But I'm using an extreme example here to show how powerful a Roth can be even if you have to convert it all at once. You may think that surely the $2 million will beat out the $1.3 million. Especially this late in the game.

By age 90, the $1.3 million in the Roth grows to $9.3 million.[18] (In this example, no income is taken.) The $2 million in the traditional IRA grows to $10.8 million.[19] Realize this $10.8 million is in two accounts: one the tradi-

17 $1,260,000

18 $9,319,405

19 $4,990,189 + $5,760,677 = $10,750,866

tional IRA, the other a taxable account where RMDs were reinvested as seen in *Figure 7*.

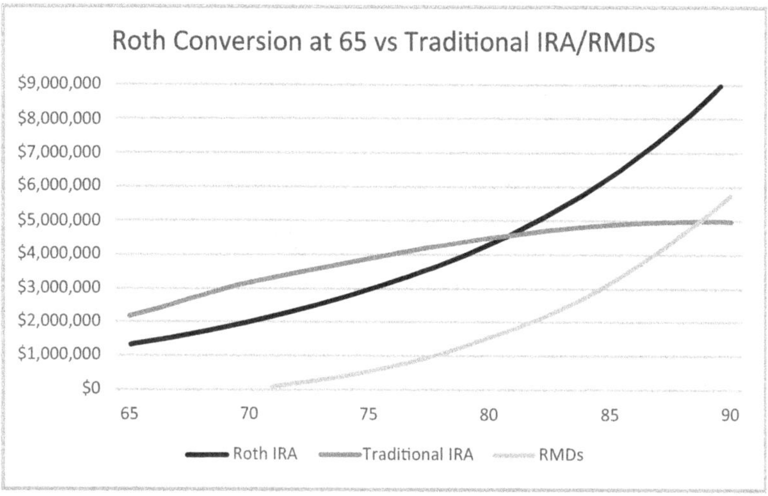

Figure 7

So for the first time in the book, the traditional accounts seem to win. But they actually haven't. Remember, the $9.3 million in the Roth is tax free. The $10.8 million in the traditional accounts still has taxes due.

Taking ordinary income taxes of 37% from the IRA and long-term capital gains taxes of 20% from the stock portion of the taxable account, you are left with just $8.5 million.[20] What appeared to be a victory for the traditional IRA ends up a loss of almost a million dollars.

20 $3,143,819 + $5,383,404 = $8,527,223

A Roth at Any Age

This is an important example. Based on this hypothetical scenario, a full conversion to a Roth at age 65, though it initially means cutting your account balance almost in half, *still* comes out ahead.

This is a powerful argument in favor of a Roth at any age. And just a reminder: With traditional accounts you have only 5½ years from age 65 to get your money out before those RMDs kick in.

Here's the real kicker! All the examples in this chapter are based on taxes remaining at their current historically low levels, coupled with the latest tax law signed in December of 2017. Take a deep breath now and read on. In the next chapter you'll see what happens if taxes increase. (They are already scheduled to increase 12/31/2025!) The race between Roths and traditional accounts has the potential to become a complete wipeout.

Summing Up

There are crucial variables that most don't think about, let alone calculate. I've done that for you. These variables often don't impact you until you are past age 70. That's why planning ahead when you are younger and just beginning to think of post retirement years is essential. You have to crunch the numbers and have someone who is reliable, knowledgeable and up-to-date on tax laws.

CHAPTER 8

HIGHER TAXES?

A Roth will protect you from the consequences of any future higher taxes on the assets in the account.

"Jill, let's sit back a moment and think about what just happened. I just showed you both how a Roth may be advantageous—even if taxes don't increase! And I used today's tax rates. So what if taxes go up?"

"But aren't tax brackets historically low?" she asked.

"Yes! And that's an astute point, Jill. Taxes are low … and they can change at the whim of Congress …"

"Well then, Will, what if taxes go back up? How will that affect the strategy that you are proposing?"

"You are right … the numbers will change dramatically. And if you don't think it's possible for future taxes to go up, there's a bridge in New York someone will probably want to sell you. I don't see how future taxes *can't* go up!"

Where will the government get the money to balance the budget? Right now they are taking in record amounts of revenue—and still spend hundreds of billions more than they take in.

Where will the government get the money to make payments on the national debt? Don't forget who is the largest holder of U.S. debt. It's not China; it's you! Contrary to popular belief, U.S. Treasury holders now represent the largest holder of U.S. debt.

Where will the government get the money to cover their unfunded liabilities? Unfunded liabilities are promises the government has made to people, without having the money to make good on those promises. These are a form of an I.O.U. The two biggest are Social Security and Medicare. The government's unfunded liabilities represent over $100 trillion!

And where will the government get the money to pay for all of the pensions they've promised (especially with increases in longevity)? Federal pensions are one of the top five largest items in the federal budget. This represents the government's own retirement account. Do you really think they will cut their own retirement? Not a chance! The answer to all three questions: higher taxes!

If taxes are not going to increase, I'm very curious where they will get the money to pay for all these things. I don't think it's mathematically possible.

With Taxes of 50%

To see for myself what would happen if taxes increased, I recalculated every example in this book at a 50% income tax. This would represent a 13-point increase on the current 37% bracket. It would also bring us back to the rates experienced in this country from 1917 to 1923 and from 1932 to 1986. There was not one year in those periods that the top tax bracket fell below 50%.

Here's a quick look at what would happen if taxes in our examples went from 37% to 50%. In the first example, $55,000 was accumulated for 25 years, but no income was taken, and the balance accumulated until age 90. The Roth still grows to $29.7 million, because an increase in taxes does not affect growth in a Roth. But instead of the traditional accounts having a combined $21.1 million (with 37% taxes), they would have just $19.2 million[21] as seen in *Figure 8*. That's another hit of almost $2 million. And taxes (at higher rates) still must be paid on that remaining $19.2 million.

---

21 $10,425,768 + $8,823,118 = $19,248,886

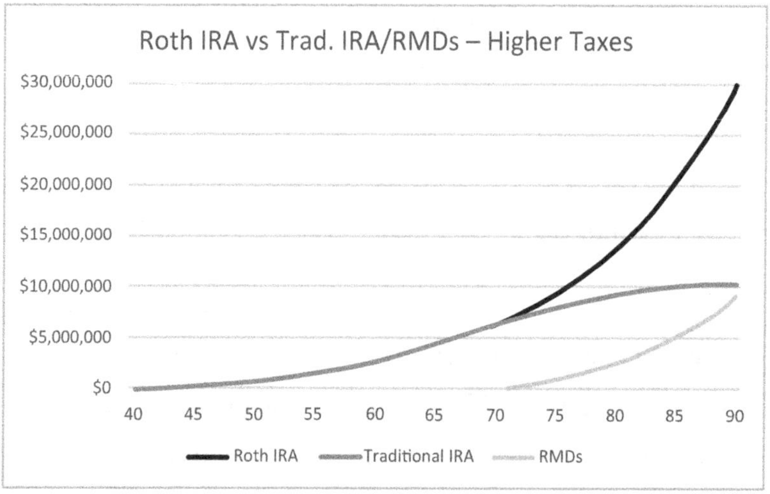

Figure 8

In the second example, we withdrew income from the accounts. Income representing 3% of the balance, with a COLA of 3%, was taken from age 65 to 90. The Roth still provides $4.7 million in cumulative spendable income from ages 65 to 90. But the traditional IRA provides just $2.9 million[22] of cumulative spendable income as seen in *Figure 9*. That's a difference of almost $2 million.

22 $2,899,264

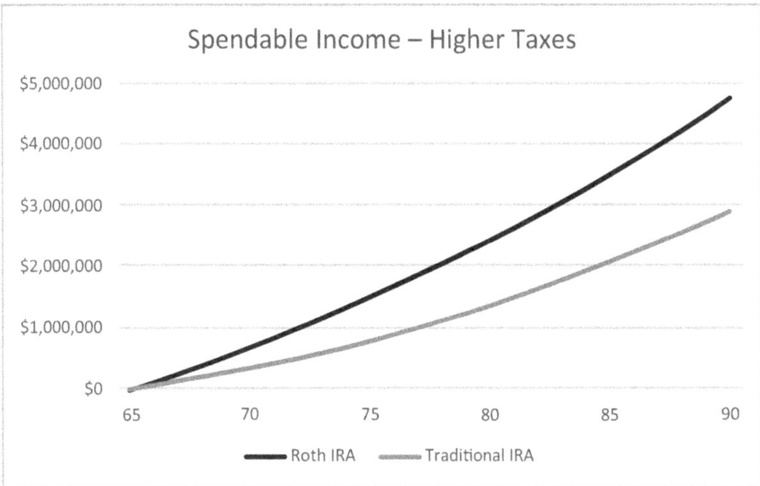

Figure 9

Traditional IRA Runs Out of Money at Age 84

In the third example, we made the spendable income equal by taking larger withdrawals from the traditional IRA (to cover the tax and leave the same amount as from the Roth to spend and enjoy). If taxes go to 50%, the traditional IRA runs out of money at age 84. Running out of money is a real risk faced by retirees, especially if taxes increase. But the Roth continues to pay income to age 90—and still has $5.9 million left as seen in *Figure 10.* The Roth gave a cumulative income of $4.7 million, compared to just $3.5 million[23] on the traditional side. And the Roth leaves $5.9 million for children, grandchildren, and charity—compared to $0 on the traditional side. That's a difference of over $7 million!

23 $3,468,812

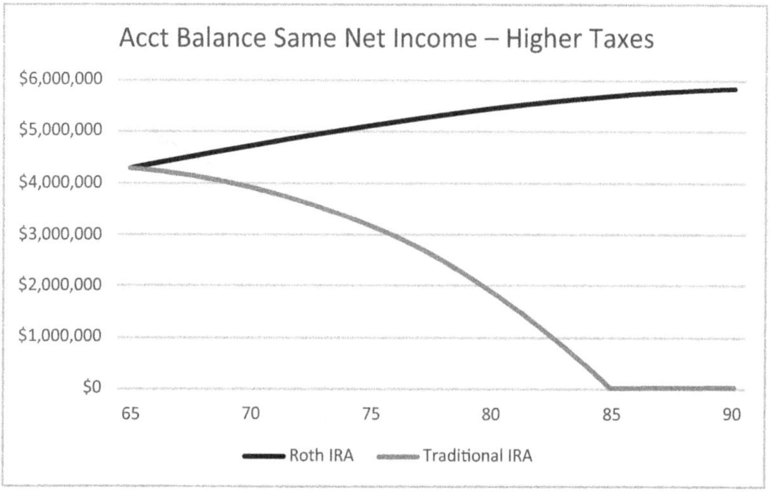

Figure 10

In the final example, we converted a $2 million traditional IRA to a Roth IRA at 65, paying 37% in taxes on the entire balance. If taxes increased to 50%, the Roth would still have $9.3 million at age 90. While the traditional accounts would have nearly $8.1 million,[24] as seen in *Figure 11,* that $8.1 million *still has not been fully taxed.* After taxes, there'd be only about $5.3 million.[25] That's a lot less than $9.3 million.

24 $4,990,189 + $3,095,679 = $8,085,868

25 $2,495,095 + $2,816,917 = $5,312,012

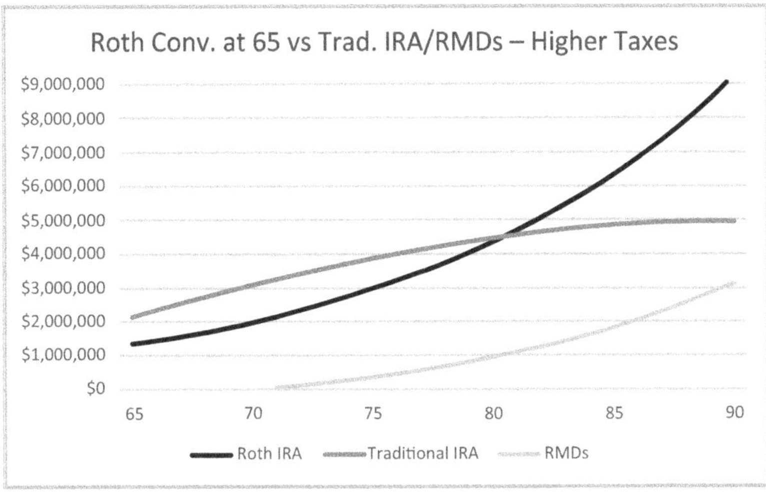

Figure 11

If taxes go higher than 50%, the gap between Roths and traditional accounts grows even wider. As tax rates climb, the news gets progressively worse for owners of traditional accounts.

After so much bad news, it's time for some good news. Let's take a look at how to navigate around those contribution and income limits that previously made Roths unavailable and irrelevant to the affluent. It's mostly potentially great news from this point forward. You see, having a Roth will protect you from the consequences of any future higher taxes on the assets in the account.

Summing Up

Granted, no one knows the future. But I know what I'm betting on—and that's higher taxes. For me, it's just simple math. And if I believe taxes will rise in the future, I'll choose to pay taxes now and avoid them down the road when they may likely be much higher.

CHAPTER 9

DUFFYMETHOD

HOW TO ROTH IF YOU'RE RICH

You now have the ability to convert your non-deductible IRA into a Roth IRA!

Both Jack and Jill were amazed with what they could now do for their retirement planning, which was far beyond anything their CPA had suggested. With the information I supplied, they were convinced that creating a Roth was the way to go.

You may still be stumped about how to do this at your income level. As most CPAs and financial advisors currently remind us, if your joint household income (in 2018) is more than $199,000 ($135,000 if you're single), you are not eligible to make a direct contribution to a Roth IRA.

Sadly, this is where many people stop pursuing Roths, just like Jack and Jill had. This section will shatter the myths surrounding Roths for the rich!

There are five main strategies for the affluent to get their income into a Roth and receive tax-free treatment of their gains. I've never been able to find these all laid out in a single repository. The fifth strategy is my own, one I've never seen in print. It resulted from studying the tax code to discover a way to protect my gains after the real estate deal and profits I enjoyed. It's a strategy you can use as well.

> **BEFORE ATTEMPTING TO IMPLEMENT THE STRATEGIES I LAY OUT IN THIS BOOK, YOU *MUST* HAVE A COMPETENT FINANCIAL ADVISOR *AND* A COMPETENT CPA ON YOUR TEAM.**

Before discussing any of the steps, there's something I must emphasize. I do not *personally* recommend you take any of these strategies on your own. That's because I cannot in good conscience recommend something without knowing your personal situation. To do otherwise would be like a doctor giving a prescription without doing an examination along with appropriate tests.

Before attempting to implement the strategies laid out in *Roths for the Rich*, you *must* have a competent financial advisor *and* a competent CPA on your team.

The five strategies include:

1. Backdoor Roth
2. Roth 401(k)
3. After-tax 401(k)
4. Solo 401(k)
5. SEP Pass-Through

The Backdoor Roth IRA

Fairly well known, this first strategy even has its own name: *the backdoor Roth*. As of 2018, this strategy allows anyone, no matter how high their income, to put $5,500 ($6,500 >50) of income into a Roth IRA each year. If you're married, you can double this (even if your spouse does not work!).

For the backdoor Roth strategy to work, you must have income. The IRS calls this *taxable compensation*. And that income must at least equal the amount you are contributing. For the backdoor Roth IRA, you are limited to $5,500 ($6,500 >50) per person. Again, only one spouse needs income (if you file taxes jointly) to annually contribute $5,500 ($6,500 >50) each for a total of $11,000 ($13,000 >50).

Not everyone may agree with my definition, but for this book, *backdoor* refers to non-deductible, after-tax contributions. Whether to a traditional IRA or 401(k) plan, any contributions made into these vehicles that are not deducted on one's taxes (and therefore are after-tax money) allow for a backdoor Roth strategy.

> **ONLY ONE SPOUSE NEEDS INCOME (IF YOU FILE TAXES JOINTLY) TO ANNUALLY CONTRIBUTE TO TWO SEPARATE ROTH IRAS.**

As you know, your income precludes you from contributing *directly* to a Roth IRA because of the IRS phaseout. Well, here's the way around this. One key piece of Roth legislation happened in 2005: The Tax Increase Prevention and Reconciliation Act, aka TIPRA. This law did away with income limitations on Roth *conversions.*

Here's the Way to Take Advantage of TIPRA

But here's the confusing part. The law passed in 2005, yet the part dealing with Roth conversions didn't take effect until 2010. That may be why this law remains largely unknown. Not surprisingly, any announcements made in 2005 were long forgotten by 2010.

Here's what changed: Starting January 1, 2010, anyone with any income level could convert a traditional IRA to a Roth IRA. The income limit had previously been $100,000, including both incomes in a two-income household! I believe TIPRA is the single most-important legislative change regarding Roths. It will also come into play in other strategies we'll cover.

Here's how the backdoor Roth IRA works. Since you cannot contribute directly to a Roth IRA due to income, instead you contribute to a traditional IRA. But here's the catch: ***You won't deduct your IRA contribution on your taxes.*** Your income most likely precludes you from deducting this amount. This means you technically have a *non-deductible IRA*.

Form 8606 needs to be filed each year with your taxes to declare to the IRS you are not deducting this IRA contribution, and also to keep track of your non-deductible contributions.

This can quickly get complicated and messy if you do not know what you are doing. I recently met a prospective client who has been going back and forth with the IRS for over two years because he attempted this on his own. This is why it's essential to have both your financial advisor and CPA savvy to this strategy and how it works.

Now that you have a non-deductible IRA, what does this mean? Two things:

- First, you have actually paid taxes on the amount you contributed to the IRA. Since you did not deduct the contribution, you paid taxes on that income.
- Second, because of TIPRA you now have the ability to convert your non-deductible IRA into a Roth IRA—something that your high income had previously prevented you from doing!

TO ATTEMPT THESE COMPLEX STRATEGIES, MAKE SURE YOU HAVE BOTH A COMPETENT FINANCIAL ADVISOR *AND* A COMPETENT CPA.

Since your non-deductible IRA contains after-tax money, your conversion will be tax free to the Roth IRA—assuming two conditions. First, there are not yet any gains in the account. This means converting the non-deductible IRA to a Roth IRA before you actually invest the funds.

Second, you follow the *pro-rata rule*. (Beyond the scope of this book, the pro-rata rule is yet another reason to "not try this at home.")

To attempt these complex strategies, make sure you have both a competent financial advisor *and* a competent CPA. There is also a simple strategy on how to completely avoid the pro-rata rule. That is what I almost always recommend to my clients.

Once you convert your non-deductible IRA to a Roth IRA, you have successfully gone through the steps required for a backdoor Roth IRA. This strategy allows you to place up to $11,000 ($13,000 >50) each year, even if your income is higher than the Roth IRA phase-out.

If you'd like to place more money each year into a Roth, stay tuned. Each strategy in this book increases the amount you can contribute.

Jack was ready to go the next step. Both he and Jill were interested in increasing the amount they could contribute ten-fold.

Summing Up

The backdoor Roth is the only way to get around the income limitation ceiling on Roth IRA contributions. Even though the law that authorized it was passed in 2005, it wasn't implemented until 2010. By the time it was *legal*, most financial professionals had forgotten about it and how to use it.

Chapter 10

DUFFYMETHOD

The Roth 401(k)

There are no income limitations, and the limits on contributions are way higher than $5,500 ($6,500 >50).

Both Jack and Jill's energy had changed in my office. They hadn't experienced the level of information that I had revealed in any discussion with other financial experts. All Jack could say was, "Tell us more."

The Roth 401(k) is one of my favorites for those employed by others. While *Roth 401(k)* is not an official designation, I think it's the best term. The IRS calls this a "*designated Roth account.*"

Created from a law passed in 2001 called the Economic Growth and Tax Relief Reconciliation Act (EGTRRA), it was long overdue. The original 401(k) was created in 1978 that deferred taxable income to a later date. The Roth 401(k) now allowed for post-tax dollars to be contributed. Once again, to add to the confusion, the Roth 401(k) aspect of the law did not go into effect until 2006.

Starting January 1, 2006, 401(k) plans were allowed to have a Roth option. This means the plan participants could choose whether to put money into the traditional side of a 401(k) plan or the Roth side. How many businesses now take advantage of this? Not nearly enough! If you are in a 401(k) program now, ask if you have the Roth option in your plan.

Routinely, once my clients understand the concept, they want in. I change the 401(k) plans for my business-owner clients all the time to allow both options. Many either do not have a Roth 401(k) option or don't even know it exists. Sometimes it's both!

Here's the best part: There are no income limitations, and the limits on contributions are way higher than $5,500 ($6,500 >50). Because there are no income limitations (phase outs), it doesn't matter how much income you have. And you don't need to go through the steps of the backdoor Roth IRA. You can contribute directly to the Roth 401(k). The 2018 limits (known as the *402 limits*) are $18,500 and $24,500 after age 50.

Simply setting up a Roth 401(k) plan for your company will allow you to contribute up to $18,500 ($24,500 >50) into a Roth each year—double that if you're married and your spouse is an employee of the business.

> **THIS IS A FAIRLY SIMPLE WAY TO PLACE TENS OF THOUSANDS OF DOLLARS EACH YEAR INTO A ROTH.**

Realize there are tons of complications that come with 401(k) plans, including discrimination testing and top-heavy testing. That is why you will need a competent administrator to do this strategy. A 401(k) administrator keeps you in compliance with ERISA and annually files the required forms for your plan and tests to make sure it stays within the guidelines.

I'll not go into any more detail, but this is a fairly simple way to place tens of thousands of dollars each year into a Roth without the hassle of non-deductible contributions and conversions, as well as prohibitive income limitations.

You just need to set up the plan to allow for Roth contributions. It's that easy.

As I explained the basics of the 401(k) with Jack and Jill, they reminded me that Jack was self-employed and did not have a 401(k), and Jill helped out when needed. Then, Jack added, "Jill has a 401(k) where she works and participates to the maximum each year."

I said, "I'm glad that you are taking advantage of it, Jill." Then I added, "Were you ever informed if your 401(k) had a Roth option?"

"What's a Roth option? I don't remember anyone ever talking about a Roth option."

Jack immediately jumped in. "What is a Roth option, Will, and should Jill be doing it?"

"First, we need to find out if there is one available," I said. "And there are other options that we can talk about for the self-employed like yourself."

Summing Up

Yes, it starts to get a little complicated. You need advice as you start through this strategy, and the employer must initially offer a traditional 401(k) plan along with the Roth 401(k) add-on option.

Remember, there are no income limitations for a Roth 401(k), and the limits on contributions are many multiples of $5,500 ($6,500 >50).

CHAPTER 11

AFTER-TAX 401(K)

What if you could prevent the gains on the after-tax contributions from ever being taxed again? You can!

As I continued educating Jack and Jill, it was clear that Jill had two roles. She did assist Jack in their business, and she worked for another company where she participated in their employee 401(k) plan mentioned in the previous chapter. She now shared more information.

"To be honest, I've never paid attention to what my 401(k) has done. All I know is that I put the maximum in each year and that it does save us on our taxes. I just haven't really paid attention to what I can do and can't do," Jill said. "Let me find out if this Roth option you mentioned is available with my plan."

"Do you want to call them together to get these questions answered?" I asked.

She nodded. "Who should we call?"

"We will need to call your 401(k) plan provider."

She made a call and got the number for the company's plan provider. We quickly discovered that it also offered the Roth 401(k) option.

While Jill was speaking to her plan provider, I had her also ask if the plan allowed for *after-tax* contributions. She looked at me with a puzzled look, then asked my question. The response was a yes.

"Would you like to know," I asked them both, "the secret of how to build on your 401(k) that few know about?"

"Are you kidding," they said, "why wouldn't we?"

The After-Tax 401(k) is one of the biggest secrets, possibly the least known strategy in retirement planning. Of course, it comes with more complications. But that has never stopped me! A 401(k) plan can allow for after-tax contributions. These are very similar to a non-deductible IRA contribution. The money is "after tax," meaning the contribution is not tax-deductible and income taxes have already been paid on the money.

THE POTENTIAL ADVANTAGE DOESN'T LIE WITH THE AFTER-TAX CONTRIBUTIONS, BUT WHAT YOU CAN DO WITH THEM.

Some people, and sadly some 401(k) plan documents, confuse after-tax contributions and Roth contributions. These are not the same. Anything under the Roth contribution umbrella grows both tax-deferred and tax-free.

An after-tax contribution grows tax-deferred, but gains will eventually be taxed at ordinary income rates.

If gains will eventually be taxed at ordinary income rates, you might wonder what the benefit is. The potential advantage doesn't lie with the after-tax contributions themselves, but what you can do with them. But we're putting the cart before the horse. Let's start with the ins and outs of after-tax contributions in a 401(k) plan.

Most of us are familiar with the annual limits we can contribute to a 401(k). In 2018, they are $18,500 ($24,500>50). In reality, those aren't the actual 401(k) limits. They're just the limit on what's called *employee elective deferrals*.

The actual upper limit for a 401(k) plan is found in a different section of the tax code: section 415. In 2018, it's $55,000 ($61,000>50). That's much higher than the amount to which we're accustomed. But since higher amounts cannot be excluded from taxable income, they are commonly referred to as *after-tax contributions.*

The amount contributed will not be deducted from your taxes, so you will pay full income taxes on that money today. Now what if you could prevent the gains on the after-tax contributions from ever being taxed again, just like a Roth? You can!

> YOU CAN CONVERT THE AFTER-TAX CONTRIBUTION TO ROTH MONEY, VERY SIMILAR TO CONVERTING A NON-DEDUCTIBLE IRA TO A ROTH IRA.

In-Plan Conversions

There are two ways to accomplish this. Again, I cannot go into all the technicalities with this strategy. Each individual considering it must have guidance to determine if it's appropriate in his or her situation. It may work in your situation, and it may not. But it's worth exploring.

If you have competent financial advisors, they have already made you aware of this. A 401(k) plan, if designed properly, can allow for a Roth conversion on these after-tax contributions—inside the plan! That means you can convert the after-tax contribution to Roth money, very similar to converting a non-deductible IRA to a Roth IRA.

In-plan Roth conversions were first made available with the Small Business Jobs Act of 2010. But this act did not allow Roth conversions on all the money in the plan. Not until the American Taxpayer Relief Act of 2013 could all money in the plan be converted to Roth.

After this in-plan conversion, which the IRS calls an *in-plan rollover*—although the money stays in the plan—the money is now Roth money. Any gains are tax-free as they continue to accumulate and are eventually withdrawn as qualified distributions.

In-Service Distribution

The other method is to do an in-service distribution directly to a Roth IRA—provided the plan allows this. The ability to roll money directly from a 401(k) to a Roth IRA was first allowed by the Pension Protection Act of 2006. Again, there was a time lag, as the Roth provision did not go into effect until 2008.

The after-tax contributions can be rolled directly to a Roth IRA. And if there are no gains, this is a tax-free event. Remember, the after-tax contributions have already been taxed. This strategy enables you to place $55,000 ($61,000 >50) into a Roth each and every year!

Summing Up

If the ability to take advantage of the after-tax 401(k) option doesn't knock your socks off in your retirement planning, I don't know what will.

Most financial advisors don't probe into what a client's 401(k) offers and what it doesn't. Most don't know the questions to ask and to whom to ask them.

I believe in *holistic financial planning*—the encompassing of the entire financial roadmap for a client. Avenues need to be looked at for which a financial advisor would never get financial compensation. For the financial success of any client, a financial advisor needs to look at all pieces of the financial puzzle.

CHAPTER 12

THE ROTH SOLO(K)

If you meet the age requirements, you can actually contribute $61,000 (in 2018) to a Solo(k) plan, all of which can end up in Roth.

This *Duffy Method* is an extremely specialized strategy and available only to a very small number of people. If you are eligible, this is arguably the most powerful strategy in this book.

Let me introduce you to the Solo(k). Most employed Americans are familiar with the retirement account known as the 401(k). But few are familiar with the Individual 401(k), called a One-Participant 401(k) by the IRS, and also known as Solo 401(k) and sometimes just Solo(k).

YOU CAN ACTUALLY CONTRIBUTE $55,000 TO THE PLAN WITH JUST $55,000 OF SELF-EMPLOYED INCOME.

The Individual 401(k) is reserved for business owners with no employees other than a spouse. It became available for the first time in 2001 with the passing of the Economic Growth and Tax Relief Reconciliation Act, known better as EGTRRA (pronounced "egg-tra"). Prior to this legislation, self-employed individuals were extremely limited in their options for retirement plans.

The power behind the Solo(k) strategy comes from three places.

- First, this method is the easiest and least-expensive way to reach the *415 limit* ($55,000 in 2018) each year, which was mentioned in Chapter 7, "The Numbers."
- Second, since this plan involves a business with no employees, there is no requirement for annual nondiscrimination testing.
- Third, the plan allows for catch-up contributions for those qualified who are 50 years old and older.

What this means to you is that with a properly designed Solo(k) plan, you can actually contribute $55,000 to the plan with just $55,000 of self-employed income. Imagine ... contributing up to $55,000 of what you make!

Here's the breakdown of how that works: The first contribution to the plan is the employee deferral, which the IRS calls the *elective employee deferral*. This annual limit is found in section 402(g) of the tax code and is $18,500 ($24,500>50) in 2018. Any employee deferrals (you are the employee) can go directly into the Roth side of the plan, assuming the plan allows it. Make sure the plan you set up allows for a designated Roth account.

Next, participants of a Solo(k) plan traditionally look to employer contributions, which are called *employer nonelective contributions* by the IRS, but are commonly referred to as profit-sharing contributions. These contributions, if made by the employer, count toward the $55,000 limit.

SINCE THIS IS A TYPE OF 401(K) PLAN AND NOT AN IRA, THERE ARE CATCH-UP CONTRIBUTIONS ALLOWED.

Here's where the magic starts. To contribute more than the annual 402(g) limit, the Solo(k) plan document needs to allow for *after-tax contributions*. After-tax contributions can then be added to the retirement plan all the way up to the 415 limit, which again in 2018 is $55,000. Once that amount ($36,500) is contributed, you now have $55,000 in the Solo (k) plan. Of the total, $18,500 is already Roth money, and the other $36,500 is some combination of employer contributions and after-tax dollars, which has the ability to grow tax-deferred (not tax-free) if you don't follow the next step.

Initial Roth contribution	$18,500
Employer contributions/after-tax	$36,500
Total contribution	$55,000

To get all $55,000 into Roth, the plan must allow for what the IRS calls *in-plan Roth rollovers*. I simply call them "in-plan Roth conversions." An in-plan Roth conversion allows you to move, or convert, non-Roth dollars to Roth dollars. Money is moved from the traditional side of the Solo(k) plan to the Roth side of the plan. This, of course, is a taxable event in the year you do it, assuming you are converting either pre-tax dollars or gains on after-tax contributions. If you happen to convert after-tax contributions before there are any accrued gains, the conversion would be tax-free, as taxes were already paid on the after-tax contribution. (Hence the name *after-tax*.)

Once the $36,500 in this example is converted to Roth, you now have $55,000 in your Roth Solo(k). And as the TV commercials like to say, "But wait, there's more!" Since this is a type of 401(k) plan and not an IRA, there are catch-up contributions allowed.

Engaging the Catch-Up Option

What is a catch-up contribution? It is an additional amount allowed to be deposited into 401(k)s and IRAs each year for taxpayers who are over age 50 by the end of the calendar year. The amount of the catch-up contribution for 401(k) plans is currently $6,000 and has been that amount since 2015. This may increase or decrease in the future.

If you are already 50 or will turn 50 by December 31, you are eligible for this special provision. If you do take advantage of it, the additional $6,000 contribution actually pushes you above the 415 limit of $55,000.

Catch-up contributions are found in another section of the tax code: section 414(v). This means that if you meet the age requirements, you can actually contribute a total of $61,000 (in 2018) to a Solo(k) plan, all of which can end up in Roth. And don't forget: If you are married, your spouse can participate in the Solo(k) plan, effectively giving you the ability to get over $120,000 per year into Roth!

Initial Roth contribution **Employer contributions/After-tax**	$18,500 $36,500
Catch up contribution for 50+	$ 6,000
Total contribution	$61,000

A word of caution—actually, several. To set up a Solo(k), you need a bank or financial institution that offers this plan.

The key to making this method work is the plan document. It is imperative that it allows for all three elements:

- a Roth account
- after-tax contributions
- in-plan rollovers

Once your plan is set up with those options, you are good to go!

Summing Up

Is the Duffy Method legal? Yes, the combined IRS tax sections allow it. Are there complications to creating the

Duffy Method? Yes, it's why you need experienced guidance. The Duffy Method enables you to truly use a Roth account to attempt to build wealth. And because all contributions are after-tax dollars and any growth is tax free because of the Roth umbrella, your net is much greater.

CHAPTER 13

THE SEP PASS-THROUGH

If your CPA or advisor is unfamiliar with control groups, you will need someone else to help you navigate these waters.

The time that Jack and Jill had planned on being in my office on a Wednesday afternoon far exceeded anything that they, or I, had envisioned. Originally, they arrived to create an IRA, not aware there are different types of IRAs. What they received was a new way to look at what they had done in the past and what the future could bring. This is what holistic financial planning is all about.

Seeing where my afternoon was going, I had my assistant clear the rest of it.

"This strategy is a beauty, but it's never discussed," I said to Jack and Jill. "This particular strategy is known around my office as *the SEP Pass-Through*. The rules and regulations surrounding it are complicated … but the outcome is potentially beneficial. What I'm going to reveal, Jack, is something every self-employed individual should know about. It's incredibly powerful … and incredibly simple."

All Jack could say was, "We are so ready, Will. What you have opened our eyes to has the possibility of being life-changing for both Jill and me — and our families."

But first, I need to make yet another disclaimer to all of you who are reading this. Never do you want to risk violating the IRS control group provisions, which could lead to losing all the tax-free gains in your Roth. If your CPA or advisor is unfamiliar with *control groups*, you will need someone else to help you navigate these waters.

The Power of a SEP

A SEP-IRA is a unique animal. SEP stands for Simplified Employee Pension. A SEP is not fully an IRA, nor is it fully an employer plan. It's really its own special vehicle created by The Revenue Act of 1978–the same act that delivered the ability to create a 401(k). With this special vehicle comes a special strategy.

As of 2018, a SEP can be funded with up to $55,000. As long as that amount is not more than 25% of your wages, it's really that easy. (There will be a slight variance for sole proprietors.) All you need to do is write a check to the SEP plan.

> **A SEP-IRA IS A UNIQUE ANIMAL.**

With a 401(k) plan, you need a plan administrator, a record keeper, and usually an advisor. All will cost you money, and those charges will come from the plan participants, the plan sponsor, or usually a combination. With the SEP, these costs are eliminated.

With a 401(k) plan, *discrimination testing* comes into play. What's discrimination testing? It ensures a 401(k) plan does not discriminate in favor of any employees with higher incomes. A SEP eliminates discrimination testing because everyone gets the same percentage of compensation into their SEP account.

What about the normal filing requirements that most plans need to meet for *compliancy*? Again, this is bypassed with a SEP. You don't have to file annual forms—a headache for most of us!

What about the typical *contribution limits* for a 401(k) plan of $18,500 ($24,500 >50)? SEPs have their own rules and open up contribution opportunities that I believe few imagined, much less know about.

> YOU CAN CONVERT A SEP TO A ROTH! AND THIS IS AS SIMPLE AS IT SOUNDS.

Introducing *The SEP Pass-Through*

A SEP gives you the easiest way each year to reach the $55,000 limit. So what does this have to do with a Roth? Most people see no connection. That's because there is no such thing as a SEP-Roth. With an IRA, you can have a traditional IRA or Roth IRA. With a 401(k), you can have a traditional 401(k) or Roth 401(k). This isn't the case with a SEP.

Because of this, this strategy is often overlooked: You can convert a SEP to a Roth! And it is as straightforward as it sounds. If you convert your SEP to a Roth before you have any gains in the SEP, you will pay tax on just the conversion amount the following year on your taxes. This means that you make your financial contribution to your SEP and make no investments with the money. It's cash. The next step is to transfer it in the form of a conversion to your Roth. Money in ... money out ... money has a new home.

Your contribution to your SEP is tax deferred. The conversion will trigger a 1099 that you will receive in January the following year (i.e., convert in 2018; a 1099 is issued in January 2019 for declaration on 2018 taxes).

This is a clear-cut way to get $55,000 each year into a Roth. And you don't need to deal with non-deductible contributions to an IRA or after-tax contributions to a 401(k). It's a no-brainer!

And if your spouse is on payroll with the business, she can also do this strategy, even if employed elsewhere. This is a simple way to place over $100,000 of income each year into a Roth.

Jack leaned forward and said, "Why hasn't anyone ever told us about this? This will un-complicate our planning for our future."

Summing Up

You can convert a SEP to a Roth! And this is as simple as it sounds. But you need guidance. Make sure you have someone on your financial advisory team who understands and has expertise in control groups, SEPs, Roths, and 401(k)s.

CHAPTER 14

HELP WITH YOUR HARVEST

You may still have questions about Roths and how they can potentially be leveraged for you. That's to be expected. My purpose wasn't to answer all your questions, but to expose you to the ways you may be able to use Roths to expand and protect your wealth.

I hope I've inspired you to seriously consider Roths as part of your financial strategy. Perhaps even more important, I hope I've convinced you to make sure your financial advisors are up to speed on these and other developments that can dramatically affect your financial future.

One question may have arisen in the beginning of this book when I called Roths the second-biggest benefit in the tax code. That statement begs the question, "What is the #1 biggest benefit in the tax code?"

I'VE WRITTEN A WHITE PAPER ON THAT TOPIC, AND I'D BE DELIGHTED TO GET IT INTO YOUR HANDS.

I'm so glad you asked. I've written a white paper, The Top 5 Benefits in the U.S. Federal Tax Code, and I'd be delighted to get it into your hands. I promise it's an eye-opener! And it's my gift to you. You can download it at *RothsForTheRich.com/top5* and it's absolutely free.

All I ask is your name and email address so I can update you with news and new developments about Roths and other powerful financial strategies. While you are there, please use the feedback form to send me your questions and comments.

One final thought. The metaphor of seed and harvest that I used in this book contains layers of meaning. In the right hands, money can produce an abundance of good.

It reminds me of the pastor who was walking down a country road when he came upon a farmer on his tractor. They greeted one another. Then the pastor said, "It sure is marvelous what abundance God has brought forth on this land."

The farmer smiled kindly and nodded. "True enough, but you shoulda' seen it when He had it all to Himself."

I take great pride in being able to help readers and clients strive to earn more, keep more, and give more. Here's wishing you an abundant harvest!

ABOUT THE AUTHOR

WILL DUFFY became a millionaire at age 33 by following the same contrarian wealth-building and tax-saving strategies he teaches his clients. He's the author of the industry-rattling book series *The Other Side of the Coin®*, which includes the eye-opening *Compound Interest: 10 Financial Truths to Protect Your Wealth.* He has earned high praise from legends such as IRA expert Ed Slott, who wrote that book's foreword.

After attending The Ohio State University and receiving his Chartered Financial Consultant designation from The American College of Financial Services, Will dedicated his work to countering the lies, half-truths, and faulty math that prevent millions of people from realizing their wealth potential.

Chances are, you are unknowingly and unnecessarily losing money to financial institutions and the government.

You are losing money in investments, fees, and taxes. It need not be this way. Will has helped people retire who thought they couldn't, rescued family estates from tax ruin, and guided millennials on the path to true wealth and prosperity.

Will spends every spare moment he can with his wife and four kids, somewhere in the hills and evergreens near Denver, Colorado.

Visit Will online at *WillDuffy.com*

Made in USA - Kendallville, IN
1145583_9781950486014
08.06.2020 0901